Bik Van der Pol
School of Missing Studies

Sandberg Series n°1
Sandberg Instituut, Amsterdam, 2017

Sternberg Press

Contents

The School of Missing Studies, if conditional on the existence of the unexplained, finds itself among intermittent, unseen faculties. In this publication format, the reader (and indeed the beholder of the printed images) begins with the traces that modernity has left us, and an edited collection of essays remains. I paraphrase selectively from key words in these essays when I say the appearance of missing questions results in learning from the overlooked, and that *not-knows.*

"How?" asks one. "Do you see the signal?" reply Bik Van der Pol, before introducing the reader to the beginning of the School of Missing Studies in 2003, and summarizing some of the key projects that locate its activities and dialogues on public space up until today. In 2013, they tell us, the School of Missing Studies became a two-year temporary masters at the Sandberg Instituut Amsterdam with a program that began in Nagele, a prototypical modernist vision of a small settlement that was built and remains inhabited today in the Noordoostpolder in the Netherlands. The program later traveled with Bik Van der Pol to the 31st São Paulo Biennial, a tropical utopian modernist metropole gone mad, and so, as a result of questions raised by listening to the Indigenous Yanomami people, the contributions of Paulo Tavares and Laymert Garcia dos Santos bring a focus on Amazonia as a biodiverse forest region, and their accompanying images mediate between laws and visual languages they encounter there with those of the West. From experience, knowledge unfolds, and whatever you do not look at or listen to, or **turn away** from, does not exist.

In connection to the São Paulo Biennial, we find the remarkably **far-sighted** reflections of director Charles Esche in "How To Talk about Things That Have Gone Missing," an essay that circumscribes the neoliberal era as a doctrine in which having no other option is a political position, and which calls for an answer to the question of: "What [...] is missing for art to play a fuller role in the production of real, social, cultural, political, and economic alternatives in the years ahead?" Esche historicizes the role of **visuality** in modernism to bring to our understanding a counterpoint argument and is generous to introduce the terms "decolonial" and "demodern" to a vocabulary that forms the glossary for this publication overall.

"My discussion of Sekula proceeds from the following [question]: What is the meaning of intervening as an artist at a site of global capital?" asks E. C. Feiss in "Collective Reading: Sekula, Easterling, and Harney & Moten." The former School of Missing Studies core tutor disentangles a **collective** reading exercise with a group of artists, students, academics, and writers that took place at M HKA, Antwerp's Museum of Modern Art. What emerges is a tightly woven argument that brings into full focus the "containerized" as a previously unconsidered subject of Allan Sekula's Conceptual practice. Script and reading are formatted here. International connections are drawn, in both Feiss' text and and Sarah Pierce's essay midway through the book, with reverence to the philosophy of *The Undercommons*, a text that is becoming more than a keyword in the glossary of many thinkers attentive to the discourses on colonialism.

Somewhat nostalgically, in "Seeing Power in Spaces," Nato Thompson reflects on alternative and experimental spaces in Berkeley and Chicago in the 1990s as key agents in the configuration of political forms and subjectivities: "[T]ransversal sites of becoming provide a collective framework for people to act on their own experiences, make sense of things, [and] try to **reframe** the world." Thompson borrows from Gilles Deleuze and Félix Guattari's "becoming," reforming it as a "becoming machine." In his set of tools for an educational turn informed by the thinking of Paulo Freire, social space is educational.

Images make missing villages **reappear** in the lecture-performance of architect Paulo Tavares, the transcript of which was commissioned especially for this publication. The images that accompanied the lecture **reveal** a layer of "secondary forest" in Amazonia, a result of inhabitation by the Indigenous people. In this description of former sites of inhabitation as "living ruins of a bio-cultural domain," the forest sits beside mud—the material earth consists of—to explain the land and nature rights of the Indigenous people. The cultivation and law of the forest becomes Law through images and diagrams.

Artist and visual cultures expert Pierce writes "As If!" from the inside of a university in the United States to call for a re-view of the academy's responsibility to speak up, "I rebel—therefore we exist." "As if!" is literally an imperative to question the past in the context of the demands of the present, and her essay and photographic documentation provide an academic view on the Occupy movement, Black Lives Matter, and Standing Rock that includes, among many other astute observations, the cautions of Judith Butler. In questioning the possibility of political change inside the academy Pierce calls for rebellion as a turn towards a new subjectivity, a frustration of categories, and as something that cannot be studied.

Regarding the intriguing description of the difference between two forms of image making, in his essay "Projections of the Forest-Land: The Yanomami Image-Drawing," Laymert Garcia dos Santos introduces us to the visual vocabulary of the Yanomami people with direct reference to their drawings, made with colored pen as an act of communication with cultural anthropologist Claudia Andujar in the 1970s, reproduced here in full color in the index of images, pages 163–175. While Santos leaves the word "presentification" unexplained, he does explain that in a pre-technical and pre-religious magical world the shaman conducts direct perceptions onto the paper sheet, turning it in circles as they "project upon" it. In a reading of the Yanomami images that relies deftly on the opinion of the revered Francis Alÿs, Santos shows that traces and marks on a three-dimensional body are not from the same ontology as a two-dimensional drawing.

Eloise Sweetman's *not knowing* can produce a *roll on roll on* effect in the essay of the same name: "Roll On, Roll On, Phenomena (Until You Are No More)." Chiming into one of the tones of this book, conditionality becomes a means of asking heartfelt questions to the reader in a personal mode of address, and this editor has been happy to see a feminist position so purposefully employed in her inquiry into the process of understanding and *listening* to and hearing the at times challenging content of the texts that surround it here. In a pedagogical approach befitting of a teacher, writer, and curator, Sweetman weaves together the stories of Bird Rose, Kulmilya, Thich Nhat Hanh, Benjamin, Jenny, Raqs Media Collective, Haraway, Robertson, Posenenske, Plumwood, and her own; Sweetman's writing is a roll call to shift power through the intimacy of *not knowing*, a **courageous act** that requires an awareness of its own **responsibility**.

Those images that reward further attention have been reproduced in full-page splendor in the index of images (161-91), selections are indicated by page number references below their captions. The glossary of terms that have been emphasized in the essays and referenced in the back of the book are for the reader to "gloss over" the many useful key concepts that the School of Missing Studies has gathered and are here offered to the vocabulary of the Sandberg Series via their dedicated process of learning through practice. The objective being the ability to see beyond the blind eye, while becoming aware of and responsive to the senses and faculties in our peripheral visions. Seen and unseen.

I would here also like to take the space of the page to thank Bik Van der Pol who have, at every step of communication with the writers, introduced me as the editor and in doing so placed a great faith in my ability to carry out their instructions for the first book of the Sandberg Series on their temporary master's programs. Our Skype conversations between Berlin, Rotterdam, and Auckland were a mental theater of understanding and listening to—to hear—the worldwide connections that they have with the people that have so dedicatedly and purposefully contributed their forms of seeing and visions. I might be presumptuous to try to answer the questions that they have posed in the beginning of their essay but in pondering my way through the book I see the signal.

Warmest,
Liz Allan

Charles Esche

How to Talk about Things That Have Gone Missing?

13 — 26

When Bik Van der Pol set up the School of Missing Studies in 2003, it would have been hard to believe that it would become such a long-lasting and accurate comment on the exclusions of art and academia. The recent period of cultural, political, and economic history can most easily be described as a climate in which "there is no alternative" (TINA), a phrase first attributed to the nineteenth-century liberal philosopher Herbert Spencer. The phrase was adopted even more forcefully by those late twentieth-century neoliberals who wanted to revive his belief in the survival of the fittest as an **economic doctrine** and **self-improvement** as the only route to **emancipation**. Over the last twenty-five years, TINA has extended its reach over economic and social theory to include full-spectrum domination as what could be termed "the general neoliberal consensus," occupying the mindsets of most national governments and states, all international political and financial unions such as the World Bank or IMF, as well as democratic political parties and mainstream media opinion. TINA has become the language of all these so-called pragmatists and realists, whatever function they perform. As consumer subjects, the rest of the people who are integrated into the world economy are faced with an endless choice of small differences in which a bigger debate about values and systems of government and decision making is stagnant or silenced.

At the political and economic level, the intractable assertion of TINA is starting to have unwelcome consequences, even for its most devoted followers, and a challenge of some kind is looming on the horizon. The neofascist reformers hold the upper hand in these discourses of change now (2016), but it may not be so for long. Alternative economic systems (such as the Economy for the Common Good) and alternative politics (such as David Van Reybrouck's *Against Elections*) are emerging as fundamental oppositions to TINA's value systems and liberalism more generally. In culture, or more specifically for this text in the professional and commercial visual art field, TINA has played a rather different role. While much of the recent production and distribution of art has conformed to the doctrines of the free market and state subsidy of culture has been aligned with private and commercial interests, the content of art has not had to adopt the TINA belief system in quite the same way as corporate CEOs, economists, and politicians. The discipline of the market has had a different effect. In art fairs, museums, and biennials across the five continents one is most likely to encounter strong critiques of liberal traditions, observe flaws in the neoliberal model, hear the voices of those excluded from the mainstream media, and explore parts of human life beyond the range of the narrow democratic political debate. This has been without doubt an important outlet for alternative thinking in general, though it cannot pass without comment that the most conspicuous beneficiaries of TINA regularly acquire those critical artworks. While we in the art world would be foolish to throw our critical art away too lightly, artists and curators who feel committed to art as a means toward developing an alternative con-sciousness and value system have to contend with the fact that twenty-five years of critical art has pro-duced little in the way of actual political and economic change. Inequality has risen, politics has become decadent and self-interested, and the media—main-stream and social—is more unbalanced than ever.

It might therefore be time to question why an artistic engagement for emancipation and justice has been so unsuccessful. While it seems that art might be the last zone of free thought under the TINA doctrines, where alternatives can be given a public hearing, it might also be that art is the field where such thinking can be safely released into the world with the assurance that it will have no effect on actual power relations. These aspects are reminiscent of the role of the jester or fool in feudal courts, where he can speak truth to the king as long as he remains without real effect. What is missing then for art to play a fuller role in the production of real social, cultural, political, and economic alternatives in the years ahead?

In attempting an answer to this question, I want to turn to a concept that is older than TINA but of a similar nature. Modernity, at least as it has generally been understood, is a creation variously dated to the start of European colonialism in the late fifteenth century or the industrial revolution in the eighteenth. Like TINA, in its real existing forms modernity posits an inevitability about its victory and seeks to eliminate other choices as irrational or unscientific. It declares anything that is not modern to be primitive or mediaeval, ascribing to its opponents an identity as an anachronistic survival that time will eventually wash away. The imposition of technological progress, economic growth, and material improvement is an unquestioned part of the process of becoming modern and this **modernity**, with its later formalization in the term "modernism," is at the core of art's contemporary understanding of itself.

One may well ask, from the point of view of a (white, male, European) socialist or a **moderate** old liberal, what the problem is with modernity, especially in contrast with TINA? It accommodates Left, Center, and Right thinking across political and cultural lines with relative ease, and each part of the ideological spectrum can find something in modernity that satisfies its arguments. In fact, modernity captures more fully the idea that there is no alternative and even bitter enemies have bought into its general theses.

Problems begin, however, when we ask about the identity of the ones determining that modernity is the only way: they are, in the vast majority white, male, European powerbrokers or those whose interests they serve. For modernity as a process is understood as being owned and originated by Europeans and their white colonial extensions. It is a particular worldview that has been universalized through crushing military power and, as the rest of the world begins to play a more active role in global affairs with the changes in the balance of power over the past two decades, modernity becomes increasingly problematic as the vision of our collective future. Above all, its intimacy with, not to mention indistinction from, colonialism is something that renders modernity no longer fit for purpose across the planet. As the world begins the slow journey away from European hegemony, and as neoliberal hegemony and the TINA doctrine are questioned, the forces of decoloniality and Frantz Fanon are likely to gather strength.

Two short quotes might suffice to lay out this argument more clearly. The first is from Fanon's *Wretched of the Earth* from 1961:

> Colonialism is not simply content to impose its rule upon the present and the future of a dominated country. Colonialism is not satisfied merely with holding a people in its grip and emptying the native's brain of all form and content. By a kind of perverse logic, it turns to the past of the oppressed people, and distorts it, disfigures and destroys it.[1]

1   Frantz Fanon, *The Wretched of the Earth*, trans. Constance Farrington (London: Penguin Books, [1961] 2001), 169.

The second is from Walter Mignolo in 2007:

> The crooked rhetoric that naturalizes "modernity" as a universal global process and point of arrival hides its darker side, the constant reproduction of "coloniality." In order to uncover the perverse logic—that Fanon pointed out—underlying the philosophical conundrum of modernity/coloniality and the political and economic structure of imperialism/colonialism, we must consider how to decolonize the "mind" (Thiongo) and the "imaginary" (Gruzinski)—that is, knowledge and being.[2]

For the future of art as an emancipatory tool, Mignolo's insistence on **decolonizing** is essential, though as art largely plays the role of the fool in TINA or modern societies, the adoption of decolonial thinking will be a relatively quarantined affair unless it reaches far into the system and its institutional behavior. While much is already happening at the level of individual artists, it needs to go further in collaboration with the major art institutions and

2   Walter Mignolo, "Delinking: The Rhetoric of Modernity, the Logic of Colonialism and the Grammar of De-coloniality," *Cultural Studies* 2–3, vol. 21 (2007): 450.

commercial structures. Here, Bik Van der Pol's work with the School of Missing Studies in different cities around the world is an excellent example of what can be done. By thinking forms of decoloniality through education and collective investigation of the world in an institutional way, through the School of Missing Studies, they point at the necessity not only to make different art objects but to shape a different art world. In response, art institutions need to embrace the opportunities of decoloniaity from the inside and to repurpose themselves. The goal must be to get decolonial thinking to reach into the cultural and political spheres, and that can only happen through the mediation of major art institutions—academies, exhibitions, museums, and collections. In the case of museums especially, they need to redirect their assumptions about history and the writing of the artistic narrative of the past through their collected objects and begin to speak about **decolonial narratives** not as deviances or alternatives but as mainstream and unavoidable.

To achieve this will require patience and perhaps some confrontations with the past. I suspect that the decolonial alone cannot carry such a burden, or that the thinking about colonialism needs to carry with it a fundamental reassesment of the doctrines for modernity—doctrines that have become so heavy and burdensome to European culture and society that it is hardly able to move. Therefore, alongside and as a subcategory of decoloniality, I would like to propose a process of demodernising museums as a way of thinking demodernity in society. Perhaps art's weakness in influencing the actual world of politics and economy provides a reason for exploring the demodern. To discuss demodernizing at this stage in politics would arguably strengthen the religious Right both of all creeds that want to reassert theocratic control. Indeed, part of the appeal of Da'esh, the US Republicans, the BJP in India, or the Israeli Right is its anti-modern, anti-secular position. But, just as with TINA, resisting the neofascists does not mean simply defending the corrupt status quo. Better, then, to use the powerlessness of the art world to develop the ideas around demodernity until the time that, together with ideas of common good and alternative democracy, they can emerge into the wider public sphere.

This step toward the "demodern" would also always be alongside the decolonial. It is a form of artistic and curatorial thinking that would attempt to unmake the modernist form and its assumptions, not through critique but through turning away from its languages of abstraction and the search for formal modernist coherence. It would throw into question the modern rhetoric of progress and the horizon of a new utopian order that is already largely discredited but not yet repsaced. It would attempt to include the peoples, classes, and subjects that modernism defined as backward or marginal. Demodern thinking is also a way to tell a new narrative about modernism and modernity in museum collections by locating modern artworks within a Euro-American modernist mythology and understanding the modern cult as a tribal cultural tradition that was enacted in major conurbations such as New York or Berlin. It would in this way reject modernist claims to universalism and the singular story of modern art's development originating in the international hegemony of New York's Museum of Modern Art in favor of pluralist forms and narratives and in acting in the present with the people in reach of each local institution.

To be more specific, let's tackle one fundamental aspect of visual art, namely the primacy of visuality in judging the quality of a work of art. This might seem to be a relatively uncontroversial characteristic of visual art, but we shall see that precisely looking and viewing, the sense that appears most quintessential to art, is, in its artistic application, a colonial trope that justifies European occupation of places that it refuses to see. Starting with the discoveries of Renaissance perspective in painting as a part of the birth of Western modernity, we can understand that "space" is suddenly understood as something that can be created on or within a flat surface and that this space is visible only as it extends from the eyes of individuals standing in a superior, privileged position in relation to the scene that is unfolding before them. The artist, or the commissioner of the painting through the artist, is in a position to make this scene infinitely pliable to their desire. They had gained control over a sovereign view that both determined the environment and had privileged observation rights over it. Equally, this virtual space was only accessible to vision. It had no smell, touch, sound, or taste, which was a loss but also a reason to ascribe superiority to the sense of sight. Such an application of vision as a way to conjure the world into existence has many implications. It allows the individual to center themselves in the world and to see space as a virtual and abstract concept, one that is first created with the eye but can later be used as a way to imagine what is not yet there and conjure it up before the eyes. This power can quickly transfer into reality, especially as new territories were opened up by colonialism in which existing forms of occupation were often invisible to the European gaze. In this way, the multiple, embodied, and rich confusion of a "place" with all its contradictions and activities can be quite easily replaced by this thin, visual notion of "space" as something that is mastered through the sight of the viewer. Newly arriving colonists therefore could recognize what they saw through the idea of perspective painting that had already given them a means to see unknown or unvisited lands. Confronted again by the colonial space of the unknown, it is relatively easy to transfer the experience of viewing paintings to providing permission for the empowered elite of Europe to see abstract space rather than embodied place and to legitimize its reshaping through conquest and mastery.

This idea of perspective, of projecting a space before the eyes, can be understood as one of the the foundations of modern European art, yet it can also easily be understood as the basis for a justification of individualism (the privileged viewer/owner) and creative power (the determination of the subject of the image). To accept this argument necessarily means that the modern insistence on visuality needs to be questioned for the consequences that it brings and that artists and art institutions need to understand the problem with colonialism/modernism in today's world.

The **demodern** implications are quite extensive. They extend from such a fundamental idea as the visuality of visual art to the forms of disciplinary organization in institutions. For instance, the political and cultural merits of the deterritorialized white cube space becomes problematic when set against the significance of the space/place dichotomy. The white cube is both a dislocated nowhere (or in colonial terms a *terra nullius*) and a simple extension of Renaissance perspective into three dimensions reproduced endlessly in modern art museums and galleries. Neither option takes account of the decolonial desire to place and pluralize our activities, and a successfully demodern visual art would have to demand a plurality of kinds of exhibition spaces, as well as a demotion of the primacy of colonial visuality in critical assessments of an artwork's quality.

The implications also extend beyond the architecture of modernity to its functions, such as education. Most forms of modernity demanded ever-greater specialization that only allowed a partial view of a condition or situation that excluded much of relevance in a search for rational and scientific methods. The modern always ignored the overview or the holistic approach, something that can be most obviously understood today perhaps in the failure of neoliberal economic theory to account for climate change, irrational human behavior, or values other than monetary ones. In doing so, it has not been able to improve human life conditions for any but a small minority, despite its best intentions.

This blindness to the whole was something that even extended to urban planning and that hugely effected the development of a colonial city like São Paulo that was divided internally on the basis of infrastructure needed for the elite class and that separated its archives and histories in ways that disable or hinder any attempts by the oppressed to understand how they fit into the wider picture of exploitation and in whose interests the city is changed. Such divide and rule tactics are continued in academia across the world today and much of this failing Western modernity is still in place everywhere. In this sense, demodern thinking, as a companion to the decolonial, would be an appropriate way to understand the ambitions of the School of Missing Studies to do away with disciplinary specializations and look for the gaps and the weaknesses in official institutional curricula, while not being certain of what is needed or might be found. It offers a forum in which to talk about the things that are lacking and a parasitical tool to weaken some of the ugliest assumptions of modern society and its institutions. As such the School of Missing Studies is one answer to how we can talk about the things that have been lost or do not yet exist but that might need to be created in order for a decolonial, demodern, and just future to unfold.[3]

3   "How to (Talk about) Things That Don't Exist" was one version of the title of the 31st São Paulo Biennial, where Bik Van der Pol and the School of Missing Studies were participants.

Bik Van der Pol

Do You See the Signal?

27 —— 52

Vision and Seeing

What is it that makes someone see or not see? Is seeing strategic? Is the refusal to see ignorant? What do we see if we turn a **blind eye**? Are we then willfully blind, or do we just believe what we see? How do we know that what we are seeing or not seeing is just, or even real? Who or what makes us see what we need to see? What do we **miss** when we do, or do not see?

Before we begin let us ponder, rest, sit a bit, and create some space, so to speak, in order to move into questioning these faculties.

The School of Missing Studies started in 2003 as an initiative of a small group of artists, thinkers, and architects.[1] Observing the disappearance of public space in situations marked by or undergoing abrupt transition, this group recognized **"the missing"** as a matter of urgency and conceived an informal, organic, nomadic, collaborative platform for experimental study and research from which to ask the question: Whose field of vision are we seeing? This school, a process-oriented and site-sensitive project, is an

---

1   The School of Missing Studies was initiated by Sabine von Fischer, Ivan Kucina, Bik Van der Pol, Milica Topalović, STEALTH.unlimited (Ana Džokić and Marc Neelen), Stevan Vuković, and Srdjan Jovanović Weiss. So far the School of Missing Studies has taken shape as a workshop, seminar, road trip, temporary master's program at a university, a research exhibition, and a residence and performance project, often in collaboration with institutions, biennials, and museums. The School of Missing Studies resists institutionalization to escape control and formalization, may appear and disappear again, and is organized by different initiators, in different forms.

attempt to amalgamate different forms of—often over-looked—knowledge, challenging anyone involved to move beyond their existing geographic and culturally based discourses, situations, and disciplines. Investigating what culture(s) laid the foundations for the loss we are experiencing from modernization and how this loss can talk back to us as a potential site of learning, the School of Missing Studies envisions a space where learning and experiences are anticipated in a continuously changing dynamic, where making public and public making are inherent to the workings of the project, and where ideas also have to be taken into action.

Contrary to models whereby publics emerge organically, at the heart of modernity lies the concept of the blueprint that imposes structures to configure or reconfigure social relations;[2] this blueprint is to be considered as the ultimate modernist endgame. But where do models fail? What is lost when we move from the scale of the blueprint to that of the planet? Convinced that we need to stretch learning (as an active process) beyond what is usually taught, the School of Missing Studies is calling for a space for loose improvisation, a space to turn existing knowledge against itself as a method for learning to think autonomously, to affect our capacity to see things otherwise, to trust that seeing and to

2   Simon Sheikh, "Publics and Post-publics: The Production of the Social," *open!* (January 1, 2007), www.onlineopen.org/publics-and-post-publics.

set one's own pedagogical terms. The creation of this space requires a continuous journey—through different case studies, **fieldwork**, and readings both in and outside the field of education—of encounters with other perspectives and sensibilities (including, but not limited to geo- and biopolitics, urban planning, and architecture), to incite a continuous process of learning in an expanded field.

Activities of the School of Missing Studies have included, among others, *Teasing Minds* (2004), a project based on a statement of neuropsychologist Ernst Pöppel that—although perfectly equipped to register differences—if the human brain is not sufficiently challenged, it will show a natural tendency to act conservatively, the logic of which was coupled with inquiries into cultural and urban developments in Munich.[3] *Twist to Wild Life* (2004) focused on the shrinking cities in East Germany as a recent occurrence that could extend to other parts of Europe; shaped as a workshop it enticed us to develop possible scenarios for a cultural turn that should not be misinterpreted as a loss or threat, but as a possibility.[4] *The Lost Highway Expedition* (2006) was a road trip along the unfinished "Highway of Brotherhood and Unity" in former Yugoslavia to retrace and study the

3 *Teasing Minds* was initiated by Bik Van der Pol, STEALTH.unlimited architects, and Kunstverein Munich.

4 *Twist to Wild Life* was initiated by Srdjan Jovanović Weiss and Bik Van der Pol, as part of the Halle School of Common Property. Results of the workshop were presented at the 6th Werkleitz Biennale in Halle.

relationships that got lost due to the Yugoslav Wars, at the microlevel of **friendships**, family, communities, and institutions, to articulate and imagine the evolution of new and transforming borders and territories of Europe, and to speculate on the unknown future of Europe as a union.[5] *A Particular Site as a Lens for Speculation* (2015) invited participants to engage in a collaborative process incorporating the many disparate languages with which a harbor "converses," where each stage in the reception, processing, and distribution of goods comes with its own syntax, vocabulary, and infrastructure.[6] The departure points for this narrative were the utilization of silence as a political imperative of infrastructure, and the role that silence will play in the future harbor, both in its human and automated state; for some, automation threatens the future presence of human voice(s) in the harbor (that,

5   *The Lost Highway Expedition* was initiated by Centrala Foundation for Future Cities, and Katherine Carl, Ana Džokić, Ivan Kucina, Marc Neelen, and Srdjan Jovanović Weiss for the School of Missing Studies. See: "Upcoming: Lost Highway Expedition," School of Missing Studies website, accessed February 13, 2017, www.schoolofmissingstudies.net/sms-lhe.htm; and "The Lost Highway Expedition [LHE]," Azra Aksamija website, accessed February 13, 2017, www.azraaksamija.net/projects-6.

6   *A Particular Site as a Lens for Speculation* initiated by Bik Van der Pol consisted of an open three-month work period at M HKA and AIR in Antwerp with artists, writers, and researchers such as Gia Abrassart, Sol Archer, Common Room, Wiebe Eekman, E. C. Feiss, Fucking Good Art, Dirk van Lieshout, Martin Schepers, Anja Isabel Schneider, Iffy Tillieu, Jeroen Verbeeck, Kym Ward, Huib Haye van der Werf, and students of the MFA program at the Piet Zwart Institute, Rotterdam.

as a result and consequence, is "liberated" from human labor). For others, the future harbor is a utopian site where humans are emancipated from the location itself, leaving the harbor silent albeit speaking in inaudible code, the engineered and remote-controlled language of infrastructure.

Invited to develop a temporary master's program from 2013 to 2015 as part of the Sandberg Instituut, we brought the School of Missing Studies inside the university. We rallied together students, scientists, artists, and activists, and occasionally scholars from other universities and organizations, along with members of the general public who became involved in different parts of the program. The program itself we loosely structured as an "archipelago," an extensive group of islands formed by both water and land. Analogous to this image of the archipelago, the program was perceived as a scattered but cohesive landscape of key areas considered to be connected in their relationship that would create spaces of experience to navigate and traverse. A space where the "in-between" is as important as the islands themselves ... a space that would form—we imagined—nothing less than an attempt to see, sense, listen, and understand what is missing ... an archipelago against relational fragmentation, while being fragmented spatially, and in time. Different practitioners from different backgrounds and disciplines were invited to each take hold of an island, taking their practice and urgencies as points of departure during intense work periods with students. These "island keepers" are working in and between

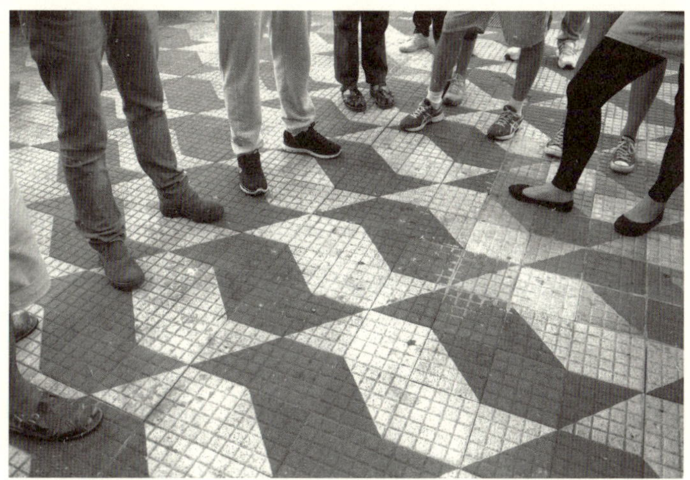

On expedition with Rios e Ruas to explore and recognize the existing 300 hidden rivers underneath the streets of São Paulo. Rio e Ruas aims to create an affective comprehension of urban space, and to see what kind of city will be left for the next generations (image: Bik Van der Pol)

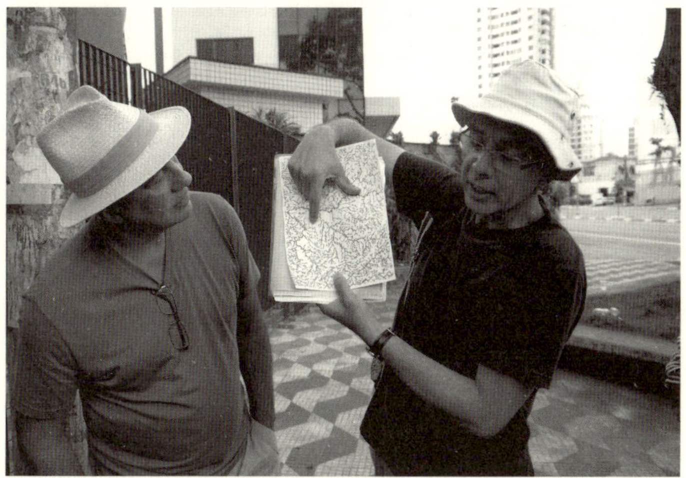

Searching for the rivers underneath São Paulo, with José Bueno (architect and urbanist) and Luiz de Campos (geographer and water systems specialist), initiators of Rios e Ruas, 2014 (image: Bik Van der Pol)

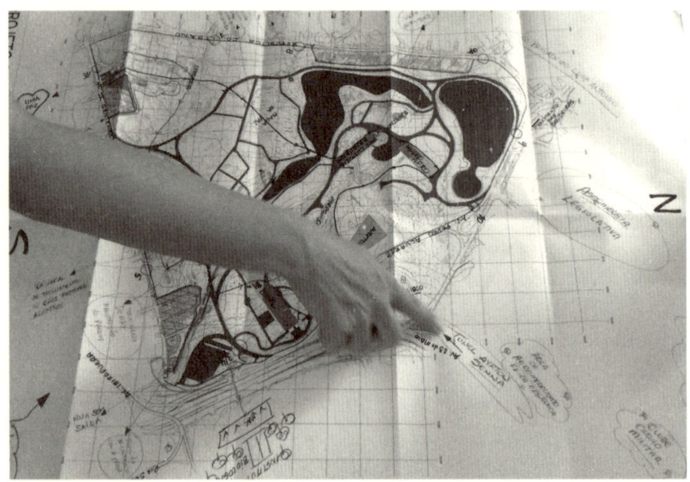

Fernanda Curi's workshop series Projeto Clima_Ibirapuera. As part of *Turning a Blind Eye*, Projeto Clima_Ibirapuera brings together theory and practice over Parque Ibirapuera's extended territory, which has been fragmented, appropriated, and misused over the last six decades. The workshop series includes archival documentation of the park and surrounding institutions and on-site observations, while investigating systems of mapping, infrastructure, and economics, and how green spaces appear and get lost in cities, territories, and ecologies (image: Bik Van der Pol)

areas of the arts, culture, urbanism, technology, and politics, in a fragmented archipelago that is undivided; as it is within the spaces in their close proximity to each other that they become what they are. Areas, in relation, produce spaces to think and act.

This School of Missing Studies began in Nagele, a Dutch modernist agrarian settlement in the Noordoostpolder and an exemplar in the modernist era of archetypically Dutch architectural planning for and modification of society. This small town and the Noordoostpolder at large, which was en-

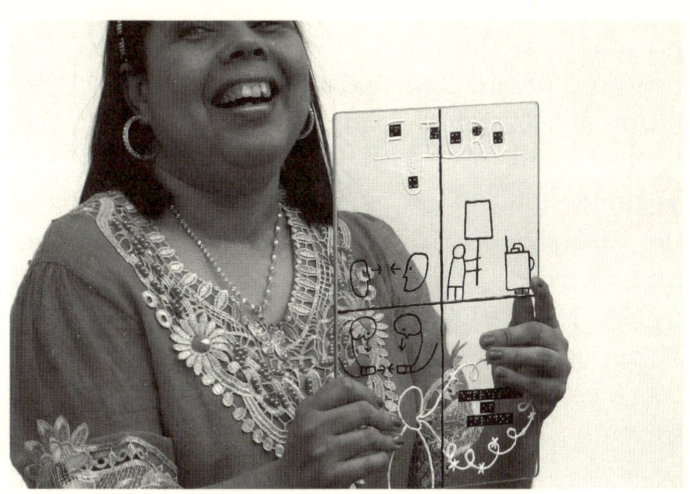

Roseli Behaker Garcia during her public talk for *Turning a Blind Eye*, addressing art and exhibitions from the perspective of people with disabilities (in her case blindness), exploring paradoxes of visibility and invisibility, and the breaking of set paradigms, 2014 (image: Clare Butcher)

tirely built on man-made land reclaimed from the **sea**, fit perfectly into the modernist vision that architecture, applied as an economic and political tool, could improve the world through **design**, thus providing fertile ground for us to reflect on the effects of **modernity** on a local and global scale. Nagele was designed by the architectural team De 8 and presented at the CIAM 8 meeting in 1956.[7] The planning of the Noordoostpolder shows a highly rationalized grid of roads, canals, cities, agrarian land, and forests, and the structure of Nagele must be understood in relation to the overall system of the polder. Important territorial principles in structure, form, and landscape can be seen in the project of Nagele; as such, Nagele can be seen as an early blueprint for the continuing transformation of the urban environment that is currently extending over the entire planet.

From there, with the help of different island keepers, the School of Missing Studies navigated from fragmented cartographies to the exploration of territories that no longer border Europe, but have expanded (in light of increasing globalization and international capitalism) into our immediate surroundings, as well as spilled outward and far into the African continent, to take one example among many others. We investigated what possible ways the

7   The Congrès internationaux d'architecture moderne (CIAM, or International Congress of Modern Architecture), founded in June 1928, was responsible for a series of events and congresses arranged across Europe by the most prominent architects of the time. CIAM's manifesto, one of many in the twentieth century meant to advance the cause of "architecture as a social art," was guided by the principles of modernist planning and was taken up by European governments during the postwar period to mount large-scale urban housing and rebuilding programs. Significantly for the School of Missing Studies, the activities of CIAM brought together all the main domains of architecture such as landscape, urbanism, and industrial design.

concept of "barbarism"—in the context of rhetoric, aesthetics, and politics—surrounds the questionable application of the term "crisis," and brought the meaningful reality of a destabilizing absence into confrontation with what such a loss means, both for certainties that we may have considered as fundamental, and for our sense of being. Artistic and political abstraction, fragmentation, and think tanks were brought to the table, and we went through moments of exposition that in turn set off experimentation, and the process of experiencing how community is formed at the margins, in the academy, and in unknown territories. The commons were a starting point for thinking and experiencing new possibilities for the concept and use of space and time. A juxtaposition of the early modernist blueprint of new towns with the concept of current and future urban ideals—to make denser, greener, and more pleasant cities that offer a high quality of life to their inhabitants—was developed by the students into a role-play and grim game for the speculative construction of a deregulated zone. The recognition of unknown kinds of human knowledge together with knowledge of other life-forms and their poetics, without fully envisaging or knowing where that practice might take us, led to close listening to understand the role of the voice in law in the face of new regimes of border control, algorithmic technologies, medical sciences, and modes of surveillance.

Being part of a two-week long encounter between six artists, curators, and writers and eleven Indigenous Yanomami[8] of the Amazonia forest had significantly affected our own view on **site-sensitive** knowledge, and was, as a kind of "lead-in," of extreme relevance for us and for how we further developed the program of the School of Missing Studies. The **practice** of mutual learning as a method of exchange formed the basis for the discussions on what learning could be in specific contexts, there, in that forest. We began to collectively ask the question of: What do people need to know in the forest? What agency can be taken in this forest? What kind of knowledge do the children who live in this forest need? What responsibilities do we all have for our different but interrelated contexts? It is hard to overestimate the importance of the presence of the **Yanomami** and other Indigenous groups in Amazonia for the survival and ongoing biodiversification of this vast forest-land. Knowledge quickly fades from our memories if it is not an active part of daily life and use, and this loss accelerates with the advent of new technologies and a reliance on digital storage to retain and retrieve data. In the case of Indigenous knowledge, lost knowledge is really lost, erased, so to say, as the space

8 In 2013 we were all hosted by Anne Ballister, photographer and founder of the Xapomi School at Puraquequara, Santa Isabel do Rio Negro, on a small compound along the Rio Marauiá in the middle of the forest of Amazonia, three days sailing from Manaus.

in which it is created and practiced, the complex ecosystem of Amazonia is vanishing rapidly through globally accelerating exploitation and the mining of resources by corporations in close collaboration with local governments. Next to the climate change caused by these activities and the loss of other ways of life, intellectual and cultural knowledge such as that based in the human interrelationship with nature, of site-sensitive and extremely specialized learning methods, of the medical qualities of plants, or local languages—are rapidly disappearing. The Yanomami and the many other groups inhabiting Amazonian territories rightfully insist on voicing their explicit and expert role in this complex ecosystem as cultivators, guards, caretakers, and indispensable carriers of culture, experience, and valuable knowledge. By resisting the governmental demand to bring their children to a school with Brazilian education they refuse to allow them to become "normalized." In fact, they refuse to participate in an active act of erasure. If we are in agreement that the ideology of capitalist society is fundamental to social control, then education is instrumental in transmitting this ideology; and then education is an ideological state apparatus that helps the ruling ideology continue in order to justify the capitalist system. By deciding that another kind of learning is needed, in their context, where they live, the Yanomami make visible what is missing from "our world," namely, a continuous questioning of what and how, and from whom we want or need to learn.

To open up new horizons of action, production, and reflection, and informed by this previous experience, we implemented the educational model of *the school* as a form of "mental theater" into the 31st São Paulo Biennial,[9] shaping that situation to act both as the site of creation and research, as well as an amplifier for solicited responses thus taking practice, as an activity, into the public arena. This project, titled *Turning a Blind Eye* (2014),[10] departed from recent

9   We borrowed this term from Byron, and Bertold Brecht after him, who emphasized the need for a "mental theater" as an activist approach to recast and restage reading, subject, and dialogue within different contextual horizons. From these stagings and restagings a social body of meanings would develop. We apply this as a form for bringing together different voices, experiences, and artistic languages in dialogue. For more on mental theater, see Jerome McGann, "The Apparatus of Loss: Bruce Andrews' Writing," in *The Point Is to Change It: Poetry and Criticism in the Continuing Present* (Tuscaloosa: University of Alabama Press, 2007).

10   The expression "turning a blind eye" is derived from an anecdote that established the terms "Nelsonian knowledge" or "willful blindness," used in law when a person seeks to avoid civil or criminal liability for a wrongful act by intentionally putting himself in a position where he will be unaware of facts that would render him liable. The British naval officer Admiral Horatio Nelson was notorious for his leadership, strategy, and unconventional tactics. He had also lost an arm and the sight in one eye during combat, contributing to his mythical status. During the Battle of Copenhagen (1801) his cautious commander sent a signal via the customary system of signal flags to Nelson's forces, suggesting they withdraw. When the more aggressive Nelson was directed to the signal, he lifted his telescope to his blind eye and said, "I really do not see the signal!" and continued the attack, risking defeat but resulting in a victory for the British fleet. The winner is always right...

events in Brazil and broader trends worldwide;[11] it was also a public program (in which students of the School of Missing Studies and universities, and organizations in São Paulo were actively involved) shaped as a series of public workshops, interactions, lectures, and "expeditions," which encompassed the experience of meaning and appearance in a place marked by tensions arising from intense and rapid growth and the corresponding accelerating exploitation of nature. The School of Missing Studies set off to trace, reflect, and register the "unseen"—not only what we cannot see, but what we will not see, or refuse to see.

So, Do You See the Signal? Really?

Let's sketch the lay of the land.[12] We can all see that we are caught in a period of abrupt transition. Recent occupations of public squares worldwide, the "cap-

11   Beginning in April 2013, protests against increases in public transport prices in some Brazilian cities grew into large demonstrations against other issues such as widespread government corruption, racism, police brutality, and the funding of major sport events in contrast to decreases in infrastructure, education, health care, and other public services. By mid-June, the movement had grown to become Brazil's largest since the 1992 protests, and it continues today. These demonstrations followed the revolutionary wave of the Arab Spring in many countries such as Tunisia, Egypt, Libya, Syria, and Turkey.

12   Used here to mean the facts of a situation; the way in which the features or characteristics of an area present themselves; the current situation or state of affairs under consideration.

turing" of private information, the dissemination of counterfeit information, the loss of the boundary between **public and private**, the large flows of refugees escaping war and climate change demonstrate the urgency of the question of "the public" as a site of conflict over rights, information, access, relations, and **objects**. It is clear that the fundamental properties of democracy, of sharing space, resources, and means have to be rearticulated, as they appear to be just as precarious as nature in being threatened by a predatory economy. Undoubtedly, changes are taking place, either unseen, or in full light, and perhaps even with a lot of noise added for maximum disarray. Signals hide, but they also appear, often in rupture.

If public space is to be understood as everything that holds the fabric of experience-as-community together, it is also this space that is violated from within, under the pressure of the neoliberal economic project, by exclusions, privileged **access**, and disinformation to the point that it is imploding and becoming invisible, a place where it is increasingly impossible to decide what is true or false. Whether public space is lost, called outmoded, or dismissed, our (re)articulation and renegotiation of it is more urgent than ever, so that communities formed by and through the events sketched above can enter the order of the political. A refusal or inability to recognize this urgency leads to a general **loss** of rights, and this loss is a real loss, with vast implications for citizens and noncitizens, humans, animals, and other species, on an equally vast, global scale.[13] Of course all this loss of public space also intrinsically relates to the loss of our freedoms—for example of speech, movement, and expression—and, by extension, to urban, sociocultural, and economic developments. It is obvious that we need new **sensibilities** to seed new formations of learning and (un)knowing toward ways of rehabilitating and sustaining a truly public space.[14]

But is public space a useful term? A lot has been said and written about public space, often in a way that does not lead to clarity. The public has been variously located in the domain, arena, realm, sphere, publicity … showing that the space where "public" manifests itself is not limited to physical space. A space can be defined as "a continuous area or expanse that is free, available, or unoccupied."[15] We propose to define space as that which is being formed, becoming through occurrence, unfolding in terms of its very meaning, which is "to meet, or meet in

13   Rosalyn Deutsche observed in 1998 that while "public" implies accountability to "the people," the discourse about public space in art, architecture, and urban studies is inseparable from heated debates about democracy and its crises. See Rosalyn Deutsche, "The Question of 'Public Space'," *iwalewa _ PublicSpace* blog, accessed February 17, 2017, www.iwalewapublicspace .files.wordpress.com/2012/02/rosalyn-deutsche-_-the -question-of-_public-space_.pdf; and *Evictions: Art and Spatial Politics* (Cambridge, MA: MIT Press, 1996).

14   See, for example, Simon Sheikh's thoughts on new public formations where action can be taken, in Sheikh, "Publics and Post-publics."

15   See the *Oxford English Dictionary* for this definition of space.

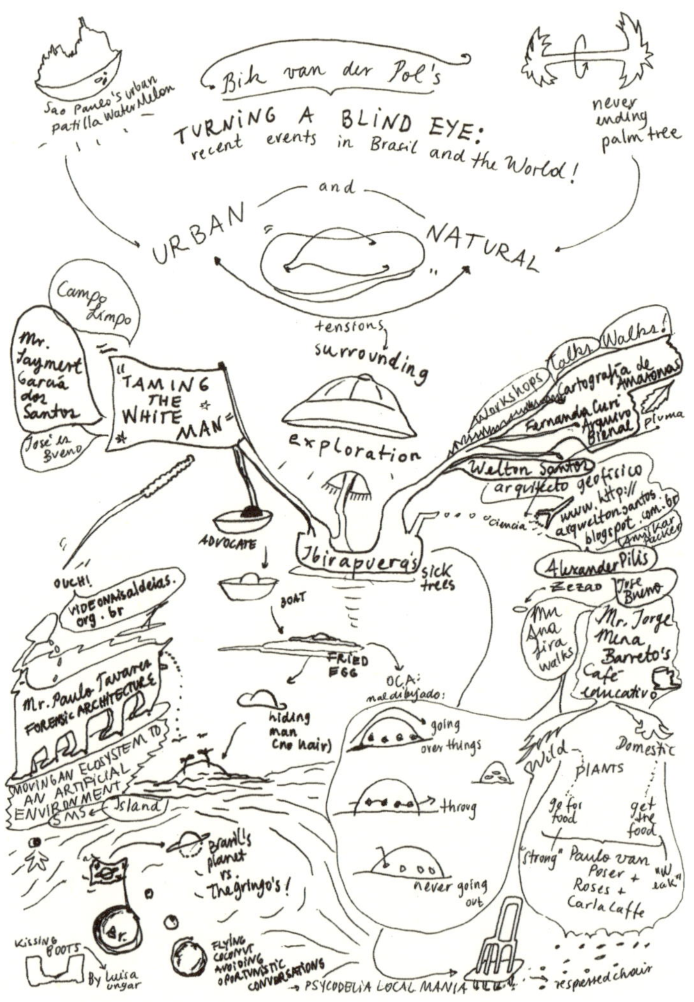
Sao Paulo's urban Patilla Water Melon
never ending palm tree
Bik van der Pol's
TURNING A BLIND EYE:
recent events in Brasil and the World!
URBAN = and = NATURAL
tensions surrounding
Campo Limpo
Mr. Jaymert Garcia dos Santos
José in Bueno
"TAMING THE WHITE MAN"
exploration
Workshops Talks Walks!
Cartografía de Amazonas
Fernanda Curi
Arquivo Bienal
pluma
Welton Santos
arquiteto geofísico
ciencia
www.http://arqweltonsantos.blogspot.com.br
ADVOCATE
Ibirapuera's sick trees
Alexander Pilis
Zezao
José Bueno
Mrs. Ana Jira walks
Mr. Jorge Mena Barreto's Café educativo
OUCH!
VIDEONAISaldeias.org.br
Mr. Paulo Tavares FORENSIC ARCHITECTURE
MOVING AN ECOSYSTEM TO AN ARTIFICIAL ENVIRONMENT
SMS
Island
BOAT
FRIED EGG
hiding man (no hair)
OCA: mal dibujado:
going over things
throug
never going out
Wild
Domestic
PLANTS
go for food
get the food
"strong" Paulo van Poser + Roses + Carla Caffe "weak"
Brasil's planet vs The gringo's!
KISSING BOOTS
By Luisa Ungar
FLYING COCONUT AVOIDING OPORTUNISTIC CONVERSATIONS
PSYCODELIA LOCAL MANIA
respected chair

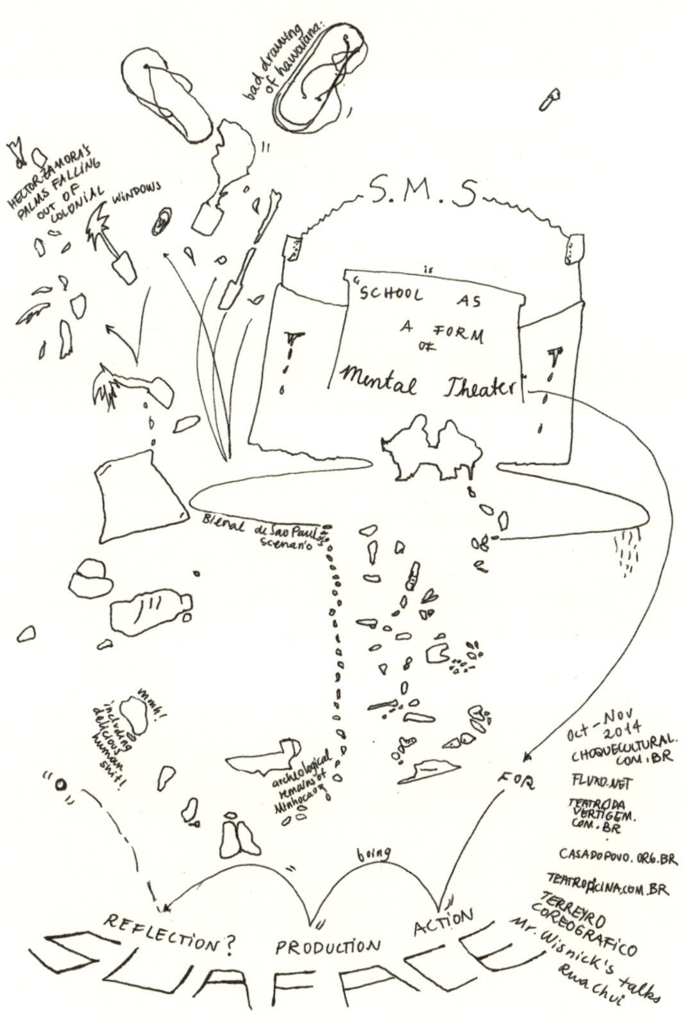

Drawings made in 2014 by Luisa Ungar after participating in *Turning a Blind Eye*

argument, to happen, to present itself in the course of events."[16] Louis Althusser evoked the beautiful image of Epicurus's atoms that fall like raindrops parallel to each other in the void.[17] Nothing happens if these atoms keep falling in parallel, but if they swerve—and no one knows what causes an atom to break the parallelism of its vertical fall in the void and deviate in this almost negligible way— they induce an **encounter** with the atom next to it. From this, a chain reaction may or may not be set off. Encounters are far less predictable than we would like to believe. For changes to not only occur but to take hold, the "right conditions" have to be present. Uncertainty is almost a given as not every rupture takes hold; there are, so to say, mistakes, such as revolutions that fail to produce viable changes. And not every encounter fuses in change; most encounters are virtual or utopian, that is, non-encounters. Nevertheless, according to Althusser the encounter is the only way things can move forward. Only then a process of accumulation and change *may* occur.[18] The uncontrolled and unpredictable energy that may

16   Etymologically, "occur" originates from "'meet, meet in argument,' from Middle French *occurrer*, from Latin *occurrere* 'run to meet, run against, befall, present itself,' from ob 'against, toward' + *currere* 'to run' (see current)." See *Online Etymology Dictionary*, accessed December 25, 2016, www.etymonline.com/index.php.

17   Louis Althusser, "The Underground Current of the Materialism of the Encounter," in *Philosophy of the Encounter: Later Writings, 1978-87*, ed. Francois Matheron and Oliver Corpet (London: Verso, 2006), 163–207.

18   Ibid., 185.

result from the encounter orients toward practice: it happens or it does not happen. It is in the encounter that the production of practice occurs, we may say.

Public space is often mentioned in connection with democracy. Like democratic power, public space stems from the people but belongs to nobody; it is a space of possibility where one can appear freely, on equal terms, unprivileged; it is also a space where the unexpected can be sparked off, a space that is continually questioned, attacked, and appropriated. Today, the use of democratic concepts—liberty, equality, and individual freedom—are being employed by conservative (left- and right-wing) rhetoric, claiming to speak in defense of the space and rights of "the people" that are, in their view, different to the space and rights of "other people" (meaning other than themselves, or from elsewhere, formulated in vague, evasive, or blunt wording as those not part of the same club, tribe, class, nation, race, religion, etc.). It is clear that public space is an uncertain social realm, fragile, precarious, and contested (just like democracy), and that this condition concerns inclusion as much as exclusion, participation as much as privilege; as seeming opposites they work closely together in defining public space.[19]

Constant negotiation is fundamental to democracy. It takes endurance and patience, and it is

19   Jacques Rancière, "The Aesthetic Revolution and its Outcomes: Emplotments of Autonomy and Heteronomy," *New Left Review* 14 (March/April 2002): 133–51.

here that it is productive to make a link to art, or artistic practice, as this involves a process of involving repeated exercise in or the performance of an activity or skill so as to acquire or maintain expertise. The performance of different narrations and situations continuously transform what might have been previously thought of as being stable or fixed, into "a practiced place" to render visible what "public" could mean and look like, as a form, as an experience where the public becomes manifest, whether through pain, risk, or celebration.[20] Society has no pre-given, unifying ground;[21] it is found in the process of doing and **learning** how to continuously form our society on a day-to-day basis.

The School of Missing Studies is practice. Practice to provoke, produce, and invoke spaces of learning as artistic practice in which ideas—that unite

20   Similarly to how Certeau understands practiced place, we would like to emphasize that we understand art, or rather artistic practice, as a verb—an active act of doing—of practicing: "In short, space is a practiced place. Thus the street geometrically defined by urban planning is transformed into a space by walkers. In the same way, an act of reading is the space produced by the practice of a particular place: a written text, i.e., a place constituted by a system of signs." Michael de Certeau, *The Practice of Everyday Life* (Berkeley: University of California Press, 1998), 117.

21   Claude Lefort, *Democracy and Political Theory* (Cambridge: Polity Press, 1991).

or separate—can assemble *in dialogue*[22]... from which they continue to develop and disperse, not as something external, but as a form of an embodied, experienced, "**passing through**"[23] (as they are taken up *en passant*: art as a political activity) in a process similar to what Jacques Rancière calls the "distribution of the sensible." Such a practice enacts a symbolic and social transformation by engaging those usually

22 Dialogue should not be understood simply as a peaceful matter. Dialogues have coincidental and specific effects as they define the basis and mode of reveal, and with respect to practice are continuously setting conditions to allow or forcefully push the unknown and unseen to appear. Much more than an exchange, dialogue is a constant negotiation between citizens.

23 "*Passing through* and *dialogue* are closely related. Etymologically, dialogue (from the Greek *dialogos*) means a speech across, between, though two or more people. *Dia* is a preposition that means 'through,' 'between,' 'across,' 'by,' and 'of,' and does not mean two, as in two separate entities; rather, dia suggests a *'passing through'* as in diagnosis 'thoroughly' or 'completely.' *Logos* means 'the word,' or more specifically, the 'meaning of the word,' created by 'passing through,' as in the use of language as a symbolic tool and conversation as a medium. Logos may also mean thought as well as speech—thought that is conceived individually or collectively, and/or expressed materially. Consequently, dialogue is a sharing through language as a cultural symbolic tool and conversation as a medium for sharing. The picture or image that this derivation suggests is a 'stream of meaning' flowing among and through us and between us; dialogue connotes a flow of meaning through two or more individuals as a collective, and out of which may emerge new understandings." See Bela H. Banathy and Patrick M. Jenlink, *Introduction to Dialogue as a Means of Collective Communication*, eds. ed. Banathy and Jenlink (New York: Kluwer Academic Publishers, 2005), 5. We understand *passing through* as a moving beyond or crossing through, for example, as making a passage, or as a journey from one place, territory, or body of thought, to another.

not involved, as we are all implicated, in a shared world; art as a political activity, where the element of "passing through" is essential because it is temporal, suggests action, ritual, and theatricality.

When political and economical forces have come to shape the perception of culture, it should come as no surprise that education—understood as a practice of learning and site of cultural production—has fallen behind. If the economic paradigm forces us to retreat from the realm of publicness, then where is the public concerned? How do we move beyond modernism while being fully entangled in production and consumption—the capitalized result of modern times? What practices and approaches are needed to **understand** what is happening today? What kind of future is already being shaped by many? Is there a future where public space survives to hold space for sharing our visions and for seeing the responsibility that exists between our islands? We have arrived in cynical times, where we are made to believe that we have no provisions for resisting the pressures from global forces that compromise civic stability. Today, space and time are controlled and defined by media. But when a free space to think and act from is considered essential, then art may well be the last niche that continues to carve out this space. If artistic practice has the potential to connect "the space of experience to the horizon of expectation,"[24] to produce new meaning and experiences, and significant change in everyday life from unexpected encounters, then it is really time to invest in its place in society. We firmly need to reclaim space for imagination where performing and practicing constitute a "social space where, in the absence of a foundation, the meaning and unity of the society is negotiated, constituted and put at risk."[25] We need to claim the time to observe, to study carefully, listen, and understand: to insist, stubbornly, on the development of a **vocabulary** of how to speak, anew. Such an ongoing exercise may not just induce new utopias or distant **perspectives**, but also may equip people with tools to participate in politics, inspire them to form new or alternative forms of political socialization, to empower them to imagine the world differently, and to act from that.

24   This phrasing was first coined by Reinhart Koselleck in *Futures Past: On the Semantics of Historical Time* (New York: Columbia University Press, 2004). He shows that with the advent of modernity, the past and the future became diverged in relation to each other. Paul Ricoeur goes on unfolding this (in *From Text to Action* (Northwestern University Press, 2008)), arguing that the space of experience and the horizon of expectation mutually condition each other; while experience never fully determines expectation, and expectation shrinks with the impoverishment of experience, dynamic tension is productive, and potentially enriching. He also argues that a crisis in modernity is when, instead of a tension, there is a schism between the space of experience the horizon of expectation.

25   Deutsche, *Evictions*, 268.

Reclaiming the space of learning as a public and politically charged space, the School of Missing Studies is a **seeding of seeds**, and its effects are difficult to estimate. Nevertheless, it is taking as its premise the potential of artistic practice (which is not the territory of artists alone) to create new formations of knowledge and action as a step forward to emancipation. Experiences have a formative effect on how people think, feel, respond, and act. In applying Althusser's thoughts on space that is not a given, not pre-scripted, but that emerges from practice, from use, that messy and possibly even violent (to shape the future we need to experience the awkwardness of uncertainty), then such a space may have to resist efficiency, functionality, and productivity, because the outcome or product is (and *needs* to be allowed to be) unsure. When that happens, and a complex process is set in motion that involves unseen correspondences between things and actions, change may hold. Architect Frederick Kiesler noted that "an object doesn't live until it correlates."[26] If artistic practices are a form of organization of relationships between disparate objects and ideas that could point out new significance to **conscious** audiences, we can perceive its role as laying out the conditions for change. There is no turning away, or back; what we need is to see both forward and backward, to connect pasts and futures. We need **multiple visions**.

26   Frederick Kiesler, untitled manuscript (1930s), Kiesler Archive, Vienna, quoted in Lisa Phillips, "Environmental Artist," in *Frederick Kiesler* (New York: Whitney Museum of American Art, 1989), 114.

Laymert Garcia dos Santos

Projections of the Forest-Land: The Yanomami Image-Drawing

53 — 68

Yanomami drawings are literally extraordinary. Not only for aesthetic reasons but also mainly for their intriguing and mysterious character. The images presented here belong to the collection of Stella Senra and the author. They were given by Orlando Nakeuxima Manihipi-Ther to Claudia Andujar, a tireless defender of the Yanomami territory and their people, with whom she has maintained close ties for decades. It was Andujar who in the 1970s brought the Yanomami people **paper** and colored pens—which they had never seen before—asking them to express through this material their world and their understanding of the world, at first as a form of communication with her.[1]

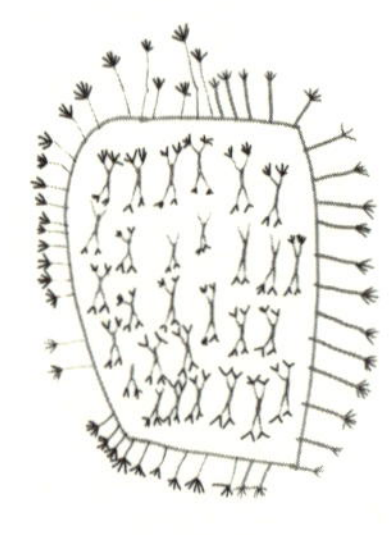

Orlando, *The home of spirits – Hekurap*

→ p 163

The Yanomami were not familiar with drawing, at least not in the way we understand it in the **Western tradition.** As noted by the anthropologist Bruce Albert, who has great knowledge of the life and thought of the Yanomami people, while their culture includes forms of expression that involve the design and implementation of graphics, such as in body painting and on ornamental baskets and other objects, these graphics are considered as traces and marks, not as images. They are printed on three-dimensional bodies and

1 Later Claudia Andujar, Carlo Zacquini, and Emilie Chamie would publish a book of Yanomami drawings entitled *Mitopoemas yãnomam* (São Paulo: Olivetti do Brasil, 1978).

objects, not on two-dimensional surfaces such as paper—which, of course, changes everything. Thus, what we see here are drawings by someone who does not "know" drawing, who never learned it and was not used to making and seeing drawings. Drawing is not part of their ontological and epistemological universe. And therein lies the intrigue and our fascination, because once we realize this, certain questions immediately emerge: How are these drawings possible? And how can this language be so powerful and expressive, with such intensity to its lines, so much balance and movement, so much vibration? In short: How are Yanomami non-artists capable of such splendid creations?

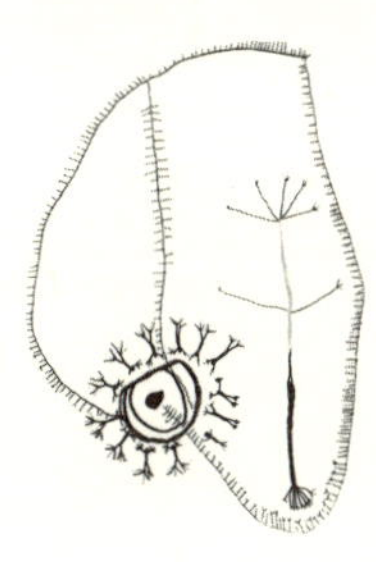

Orlando

→ p 165

The regular criteria of art history is an inadequate tool to explain the quality of this production, and to say that these drawings are "inspired" does not explain them either. Nevertheless, it is obvious that the Yanomami have direct and spontaneous access to an extreme freedom of line. Where does this freedom come from?

Convinced that the Yanomami are great (non)draftsmen and (non)artists, I wanted to check whether the high quality I observed in their work was shared by others and not just a result of my own subjective observation, or an overestimation due to my involvement with the Indians and my daily coexistance with eight of their drawings.[2] So I put my admiration to the test; I wanted to present the drawings to an artist not committed to the Yanomami and the Indigenous cause, someone free from personal bias, so to speak.[3] I had the opportunity to show Andujar's collection of drawings to Francis Alÿs when he came to São Paulo in 2010 to install his work in the São Paulo Biennial. Alÿs looked intensely at drawing after drawing, immersing himself in this universe. His engagement was evident but he made no comments, except for asking Andujar for clarification on some of the figures. When he had seen

2   I have been in contact with the Yanomami since the 1990s, initially by way of the Comissão Pró-Yanomami (CCPY), an NGO founded by Claudia Andujar, Carlo Zacquini, Bruce Albert, and Alcida Ramos, which fought for the demarcation of the land of the Yanomami, and later for the defense of the territory and culture of the Yanomami people. More recently, from 2008 to 2010, Davi Kopenawa, the Yanomami shamans, and the Watoriki community participated in the realization of the multimedia opera *Amazonas*, presented at the Munich Biennale (International Festival for New Music Theatre) and at SESC Pompéia, in São Paulo. In 2011 and 2012, on the initiative of Kopenawa, two meetings of shamans were held within the scope of the Dispositivos de Visão project carried out by the Laboratório de Cultura e Tecnologia em Rede, of the Instituto Século 21, which resulted in the film *Xapiri*, codirected by Leandro Lima, Gisela Motta, Stella Senra, Bruce Albert, and myself.

3   The captions are on the back of the drawings. Later on, some few words were spelled differently accordingly to linguistic studies of the Yanomami language. We chose to transcribe the wording as it appears in the original drawing (even when we cannot find the word in dictionary) in order to stress the originality of the collection of those drawings and their meanings in the 1970s. In cases where the original information appeared only in Portuguese, we have included the Yanomami terms as well, after consulting Luís Laudato, "Glossário," in *Yanomami pey këyo: O caminho yanomami* (Brasília: Universa, 1998)

sixty to seventy drawings he stopped, preferring not to continue in case he compromised his experience of what he had already seen. What caught his attention the most was the way a drawing would occupy the entire space of the paper, whether it was large or small; whether they filled the entire field or not the lines and figures were drawn up to the border of the paper. Alÿs found that the way a drawing by the Yanomami activated the space was radically different from that of Western drawing, in which the subject matter always exists as a fragment that appears loose on the page, rarely as a whole. Most surprising to him was the way the drawings were made: the way the movement extended through the space, taking it over completely. He thought about the process of their making, recognizing that the drawings were not constituted as compositions but as a process in progress, as projections of images that appeared configured, whether they arose from the outer world or from the spirit of the draftsman. The artist realized that the hand of those who drew and the eye of those who saw the picture were the operators of an inaugural act, the act of effecting the passage of an image that up until then had not been outwardly manifested as such, but which, upon being projected, found its place on the sheet of paper as a space to be resolved. This gave rise to the unique integrity of the drawings, the

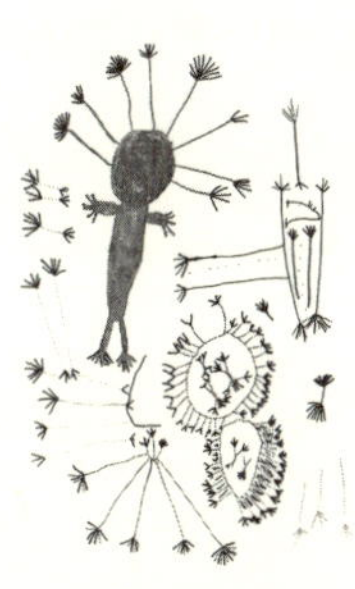

Orlando, *The home of the spirits*

→ p 167

affirmation of a totality never seen before. For this reason, Alÿs considered the drawings to be precious and unique.

The experience of watching the artist as he was looking at the drawings not only confirmed my own aesthetic impression, but also itself constituted an event mediated by the encounter with the drawings. As if the act that was crystallized in the discovery of the drawing's singularity would decipher or convert, for us as a witness to this event, a mode of artistic existence as activity wherein the Yanomami are the agents: a magic mode of existence.

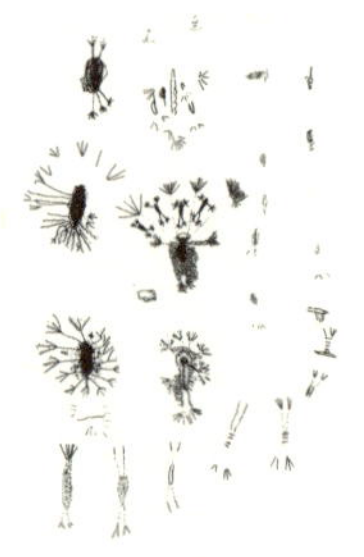

Titi, *The night*

→ p 169

The philosopher Gilbert Simondon defined the magic mode of existence as being "pre-technical and pre-religious, immediately above a relation that would be just the living being with the environment."[4] Rather than signifying a primary, rough relationship that would be "surpassed" by the end of the magical phase and the advent of other, later modes of existence, the magic mode of existence signifies a primeval human- world relationship, an original and most intimate relationship that can be developed between the human and the environment, as opposed to a separation that detaches the figure from

4   Gilbert Simondon, *Du mode d'existence des objets techniques* (Paris: Aubier-Montaigne, 1969), 156. My translation.

the background. For this very reason the magical mode of existence is characterized as a process of metamorphosis: a flow, a continuum of transformations and individuations in which the past, present, and process of becoming are in coexistance. It is a mode of existence in which the tensions and powers of the virtual act together, produce meaning, and are actualized by contact and transmission, by "disparation,"[5] information, and invention.

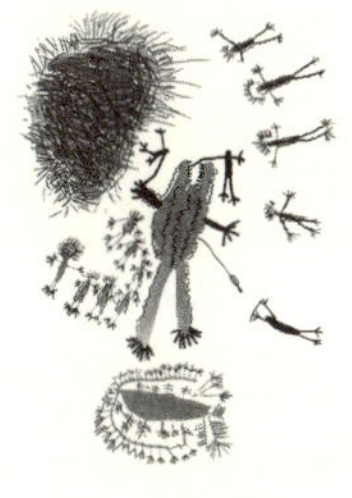

Orlando, *Revenge of Sihirim*

→ p 171

The **reader** who is also a **viewer** can, on his own, see how the magical mode of existence functions in the Yanomami image-drawings and how magical thought is expressed in the captions accompanying them (most of them recorded by Carlo Zacquini). These captions function not to explain the drawings but rather to imply what is happening in this real-time flow, **captured** and **projected** on the paper. The reader-viewer needs to understand that the language expressed by magical thinking does not represent the magical mode of existence of the image-drawings, just as these drawings, in turn, do not represent an existing reality outside of themselves. Indeed, we are not in any way in the field of representation, but rather in what Gilles Deleuze and Félix

5   Ibid. With "disparation" Simondon refers to being never in a single homogenous reality, but instead as existing in two ordered states of disparation, meaning the realms from which new "entities" emerge.

Guattari denominated as the "wild material-semiotic regime of signs, whose socius is Earth."[6] Therefore, when contemplating the drawings, one must take into account that their motif is what the Yanomami call the *forest-land*.

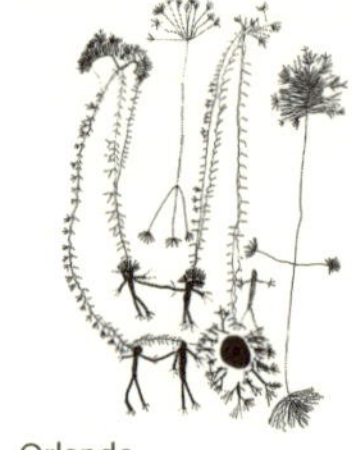

Orlando

→ p 173

The term forest-land cannot and should not be confused with the meaning we assign to the word "land," and therefore it cannot be translated as such. There is an unbridgeable ontological and epistemological difference between them, and this difference prevents the land from being objectified and appropriated by humans, a process by which they, in turn, become subject to separation, detached from it, and, as a result, aloof and hostile to it. In his text in *Yanomami: L'Esprit de la foret*, Albert clarifies how the Yanomami understand "forest":

> In the Yanomami language the word *urihi* both denotes the rainforest and the soil on which it extends. It also refers, by successive links, to an idea of open and contextual territoriality. Thus, the expression *ipa urihi*, "my forest-land" can

6   Gilles Deleuze and Félix Guattari, *L'Anti-Œdipe: Capitalisme et schizophrénie* (Paris: Éditions de Minuit, 1972). My translation.

denote the region of birth or current residence of a speaker (such as use of domain), while *yanomae thëpë urihipë*, "the forest-land of human beings (Yanomami)" comes closer to our idea of "Yanomami territory" and *urihi a pree*, "the great forest-land" refers to an all-encompassing space that echoes our concept of "earth." As an inexhaustible reservoir of resources indispensable to their existence, this "forest-land" is not, however, in no way to the Yanomami an inert and mute setting outside society and culture, an inanimate nature that is subject to human will and exploitation. Rather, it is a living entity endowed with a shamanic spirit-image (*urihinari*), a vital breath (*uixia*), and power of immanent growth (*në rope*). Moreover, it is animated by a complex dynamics of exchanges, conflicts and transformations between the different categories of beings— human and non-human, visible and invisible—that inhabit it.[7]

7   Bruce Albert, Davi Kopanewa et al., *Yanomami: L'Esprit de la forêt* (Paris: Fondation Cartier pour l'art comtemporain, 2003), 46. My translation.

This forest-land involves therefore a real and a virtual dimension in constant interaction, which do not seem to allow a separation between the transcendent and immanent planes,[8] at least as we understand them, since transcendence and immanence are part of the "same economy of metamorphoses," to use Albert's expression. In this sense, the forest-land cannot be confused with a landscape, a "medium" or objectified area as a mere source of resources whose existence is only justified because it can provide humans with survival or enrichment. The meaning of the forest is not in any way one-dimensional. For this reason, the words of the shaman complement those of the anthropologist:

What you call nature, is *urihi*, the forest-land in our language, and its image that the shamans see, is the *urihinari*. The existence of this image is what makes the trees live. What we call *urihinari* is the spirit of the forest: the spirits of the trees (*huutihiripë*), of the leaves (*yaahanaripë*), and the lianas (*thoothoxiripë*). These spirits are many and play on the forest floor. We also call them *urihi*, nature, as well as the animal spirits, the *yaroripë*, and even the bees, the turtles, and the snails.

8   Ibid. A level of existence, thought, or development.

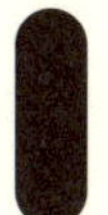

The forest's fertility, *në rope*, is also nature for us: it was created with this; it is its wealth.[9]

Land, forest, humans, spirits, animals, and plants are thus to be understood within the meaning of the **forest-land**. This is what is present in the Yanomami image-drawings. But there is still one thing that the reader-viewer should be aware of, that is the status of the image in the Yanomami cosmology and culture. As shaman Davi Kopenawa mentions, it is essential to understand the role of the image in shamanism, because the image-drawings match and hold a very strong resonance with what the shamans see during their rituals. Also, it is necessary to stress that many Yanomami **draftsmen** are either shamans, or sons of a shaman. Finally, it should be noted that literacy, even in their mother language, brings about an interference in the lines of the drawings, which is not the case of the drawings seen here.

What is the image in Yanomami shamanism? Albert writes:

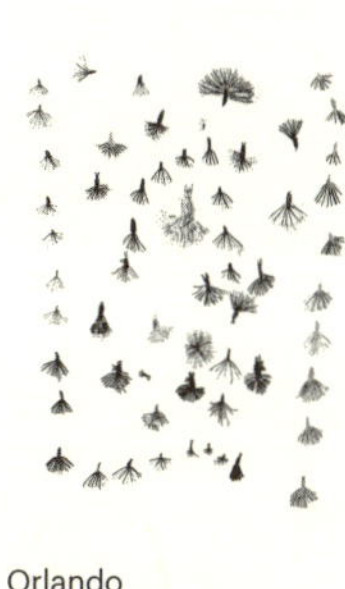

Orlando

→ p 174

9   Davi Kopenawa, "Urihi a," in *Yanomami: L'Esprit de la forêt*, 51. My translation.

The images (*utupë*) that the Yanomami shamans "invoke," "bring down" and "make dance"—during the dream or trance—are (essentially but not exclusively) those of "humanimals, ancestors living in times of origins...." It is said that such images constitute the "specter value" of the primordial beings endowed with a human "skin" (body) and with an animal name (identity). The shamans perceive them in the form of an infinite multiplicity of tiny humanoids, adorned with body paint and ornaments of dazzling light. Such corpuscular image-beings, sorts of mythological beings, inhabit the world in a free state, caught up in a ceaseless activity of games, exchanges and wars that sustain the dynamics of the visible phenomena. Once installed during the initiation in a celestial dwelling associated with the young shaman, they become his "sons," a "kindred" form of humanimal images of the "first time." They are then, according to the ethnographic jargon, "auxiliary spirits" (*xapiri pë*). Once the *xapiri pë* are domesticated in this way they are selected and combined in each shamanic session, according to their attributes and skills.[10]

According to Albert, this fundamental notion of the image-being constitutes the center of gravity in Yanomami ontological and cosmological thought. The anthropologist also points out that the shamanic images—dreamed or induced by hallucinations—should not be classified as what we call "mental images" (such as mirages or inner visions), as they are described by the shamans as direct perceptions of an absolutely tangible outer reality. On the other hand, Albert insists, "this is not a phenomenon of representation, but rather a process for the presentification of the invisible [...]. Neither replicas, nor metaphors, the *utupë* images are first of all ontological states whose intermittent visibility is made effective during the shamanic session by an effect of corporal transduction."[11]

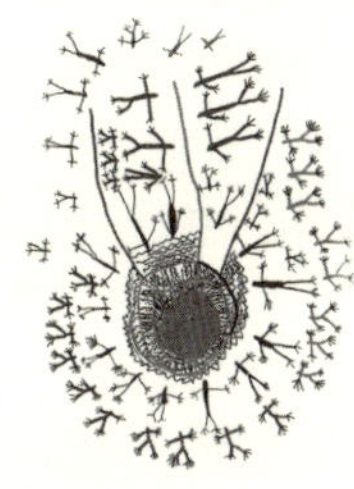

Orlando, *Motoka and sons*

→ p 175

Everything takes place, then, as if the Yanomami image-drawings were configured as projections of the capture of utupë images that non-

10   Bruce Albert, "Images, traces et 'hyper images' : impromptu d´ethnographie noctambule in imagine ambulat homo Augustin," *La Trinité, livre XIV* 4, no. 6: 1. My translation.

11   Ibid. Presentification is a philosophical concept meaning the event of becoming present.

shamans and non-Yanomami can have access to, because instead of coming down and passing through the shaman's body without leaving a trace, they do this coupled to an expressive device that can make their occurrence visible and recordable. This does not mean to say that the image-drawings are the utupë images. These we will never see; they remain inaccessible. But we can consider the image-drawings as their echo, an echo of their passage.

Becoming visible, being projected in the blank space, the image-drawings inscribe the forest-land onto a surface that transfigures through the sheet of paper, taking it to the limit of its topology. Indeed, in addition to the magic—or rather, because of it—the Yanomami drawings make us think and raise a disturbing question. This is what transpires in the philosophical reflections of David Lapoujade, during our conversations in Watoriki, when he spoke of the multiplicity of perspectives that give consistency to the image:

> Returning to the drawings, there is a question that cannot be considered only in light of the real and the virtual. Something that seems very important to me, that also Bruce briefly mentioned: it is the image ... and the fact that it is impossible, from the point of view of the coexistence of perspectives that are incompatible

in terms of representation. And these incompatibilities that are, nevertheless, in the smallest drawing, seem very rich to me, perhaps even richer than the questions of real-versus-virtual, whole-versus-part, or questions of power. Because insofar as these planes coexist, this coexistence of perspectives "arranges" them in relationship with each other: the perceptual plane with the cosmological plane, with the intensive plane and with … not the representative, but figurative plane, that is, more precisely, vision, in shamanic states. If there is something that Western art never knew how to do, despite all its audacity, it is this sort of thing [...]. We are interested, first of all, in this insertion at the border of topology (as they are incompatible spaces) that is, it seems to me, the most startling and innovating, as well as what is the uttermost breaking with Western art.[12]

12   Stella Senra, "Conversações em Watoriki: Das passagens de imagens às imagens de Passagem; Captando o audiovisual do xamanismo," *Cadernos de Subjetividade* 8, no. 13 (October 2011): 76. My translation.

Listening to Lapoujade, Albert adds that the drawings are a multi-perspectivist spontaneous agglomeration, that the entire Yanomami territoriality is a cluster of viewpoints, and that everything is interconnected and interwoven, embedded in a multiplicity of spatial and temporal perspectives. Reiterating that this is effectively a **topology**, Lapoujade concludes: "So, it means that there is never a single image [...]. There are always various images. We should actually call it 'multi-image.'"[13]

These comments about the relevance of the topological question reiterate Alÿs's observations on how the drawing occupies space. And this becomes even more relevant when Carlo Zacquini, who saw Taniki and Koromani in the process of making their drawings, reports that the vertical or horizontal position of their drawings usually has no importance; while making them they turn the paper all the time, giving the observer the impression that the drawing is being made upside down and right way up again.

"Projections of the Forest-Land: The Yanomami Image-Drawing" was first published in Moacir dos Anjos, ed., *Caderno Sesc_Videobrasil 8: Belong* trans. John Norman and Bruno Gambarotto (São Paulo: SESC, 2012), 55–68. Edited for this occasion by Bik Van der Pol. Drawings courtesy of the collection of Laymert Garcia dos Santos and Stella Senra. In addition to those referenced above, the following texts have been very important in the writing of this essay: Albert Bruce, *La chute du ciel: Paroles d'un chaman Yanomami* (Paris: Terre Humaine Plon, 2010) and "Taniki" and "Joseca," in *Histoires de Voir* (Paris: Fondation Cartier pour l'art contemporain, 2012); and Comissão Pró-Yanomami, *Yama ki hwërimamouwi thë ã oni: Palavras escritas para nos curar* (Watoriki: CCPY/MEC/PNUD, 1997).

13   Ibid.

E. C. Feiss

Collective Reading: Sekula, Easterling, and Harney & Moten

69 — 86

The following is the script from an exercise in collective reading that took place at the Museum of Modern Art in Antwerp (M HKA) on January 5, 2016. At the invitation of the School of Missing Studies, I developed this collective reading exercise to take place as part of LODGERS, a public program initiative with AIR Antwerp in M HKA's top-floor galleries. Some sections of the text were read collectively, other parts I delivered as a lecture. The LODGERS program as a whole sought to consider what relation art (as a set of practices and marketable objects) might have to the historic port of Antwerp, a vestibule between the dematerialization of finance and the ongoing circulation of goods internationally. Allan Sekula's practice served as a departure point, both because of his focus on maritime trade and because his work, *Ship of Fools / The Dockers' Museum* (2010–13), had recently been acquired by M HKA. The work of its archiving had spurred two PhD studentships at the University of Leuven (KU Leuven, or Katholieke Universiteit Leuven), and the contemporaneous unfolding of this institutionalization hung over the larger question of art in proximity to the port.

Part I: Introduction

My discussion of Sekula proceeds from the following question: What is the meaning of intervening as an artist at a site of global capital? In this case the site is a port and we are talking about maritime trade. Many art works have been made about Wall Street, auction halls, banks, and the factory, of course. What distinguishes a port from these, in its particular conditions of labor, production, circulation, and daily operation?

We'll be reading passages from Keller Easterling's *Enduring Innocence* and Stefano Harney and Fred Moten's *The Undercommons* in relation to Sekula's practice.[1] All three, in different respects, offer up *containerization* as a process of logistics, which allows us to tie art practice to the functioning of the port. My rationale for choosing these particular texts is as follows.

Easterling situates the container as a "spatial product": a form that makes the larger manifestation of the port possible. Harney and Moten link contemporary logistics to the container space of the slave *ship*. They historicize the theory around containerization as anything but a contemporary phenomenon, foregrounding our relation here (in this museum, as practitioners, at the site of the port) to the history of slavery as a necessary referent in our critique of capitalism and offering a crucial theory of containerization as part of the production of subjectivity. Thus they remind us that whatever critique of capital we develop at the site of this port, there are differential degrees of violence at stake. Undergirding Easterling's book is a sustained analysis of how the dematerialization of a single

1   Keller Easterling, *Enduring Innocence: Global Architecture and Its Political Masquerades* (Cambridge, MA: MIT Press, 2005) and Stefano Harney and Fred Moten, *The Undercommons: Fugitive Planning & Black Study* (New York: Minor Compositions, 2013).

source of authority, rephrased here as the **eradication** of authorship, is a process of depoliticization in the freetrade zones she analyzes. Harney and Moten rather, understand this movement of system eclipsing subject, the eradication of the author in Easterling's account, as the desire to **exterminate** a certain subject, as a violent force.

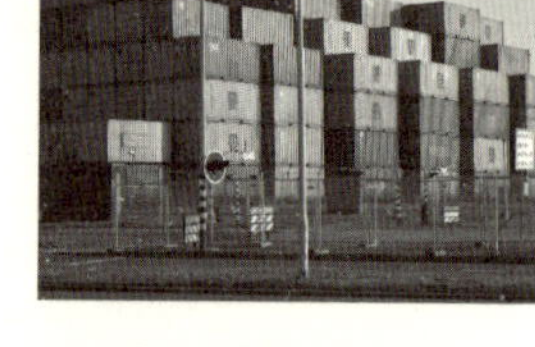

Rotterdam harbor, 2016
(image: Bik Van der Pol)

→ p 176

Sekula's practice—through its operation of (Western-style) Conceptualism—offers the shipping container as a formal element. It does this by destabilizing the borders between artistic practice and the mechanisms of global trade in the port city. This can be seen in Sekula's own situating of himself in *Ship of Fools* on the boat, through his practice's attempt at or rumination on solidarity with the workers' unions.[2] Although the photographs at first appear to be documentary, their structural featuring of the container through repetition, use of text, and conditions of display allow it to enter a space between the photograph and artistic form. The container enters the institutional space differently to how it would through photographs alone. In other words, Sekula is featuring the container as a form, a key unit of maritime trade rather than an incidental utility. In the museum this cell becomes an artistic form, rather than an objective rendering in a photograph. More abstractly, the container (and Sekula's serial focus on it) becomes blurred with artistic form

2   *Ship of Fools* consists, first, of a corpus of thirty-three framed photographs and two slide projections of more than one hundred images, all made by the artist, and titled *Ship of Fools*. Secondly, it contains a gigantic collection of various objects, graphic images, postcards, and prints that the artist purchased, mostly online. This material collection is known as *The Dockers' Museum*.

through Conceptualism's relation to automation.[3] Both Conceptualism and capital's **processes of automation**, a relationship that has been discussed since the inception of this form of art, share a desire to **displace** the author.[4] So we have the container, and we have automation between it and **Conceptualism**. These are our three foci.

Further, an animating motif in all three texts is the sea, which appears as an aesthetic element that makes possible but also intervenes in the operation of the port. How is the sea's theorization as a space of instability related to the inseparability of the aesthetic in its conjuring? This inseparability is evidenced by Sekula's *Ship of Fools / The Dockers' Museum*, in which the sea's appearance is visually sublime, even as it also functions as a historical character and an imaging of liquidity in capital within the same project.

First, I want to situate Sekula's practice as the artistic representative at stake here right now, both conceptually and materially. Sekula's work, in part, is

3   The container appears repeatedly in Sekula's work, and not only because it populates the environments he had focused on; he featured it. For another example, see the first image of the trailer for the film essay "The Forgotten Space" (2010), uploaded by Icarus Films, October 17, 2013, www.vimeo.com/77155362.

4   Writing in the introduction to one of her "numbers shows" in 1969, a series of exhibitions that helped define the North American style of Conceptualism, Lucy Lippard links the historical trajectories of artistic Conceptualism to the automation of labor: "When automation frees millions of hours for leisure, art should gain rather than diminish in importance." Lucy Lippard, "Introduction to 557, 087," in *Conceptual Art: A Critical Anthology*, ed. Alexander Alberro, Blake Stimson (Cambridge, MA: MIT Press, 1999).

a canonical representative of Conceptual photographic practice; he deploys a relation between image and text that attempts to destabilize the historic authority of both systems as a project of capitalist critique. The finer points of the distinction between postwar Conceptualism proper (works of the late 1960s) and later Conceptualist intervention into photography must be nuanced elsewhere.[5] However, it is worth generally sketching the field as one where Sekula inherited the text/image juxtaposition and the serial methods of framing and display as a project of critique, from the earlier moment of Conceptualism. Later works of Conceptual photographic practice (such as the 1980s work of Jeff Wall as a prominent example) contemporary with Sekula's, have predominately been understood as interventions into photography, and theorized as such. Important for our purposes; this meant that Sekula was able to both situate himself as present in the work (perhaps unlike linguistic Conceptualists of the earlier era, whose text works could manifest further away from their bodily selves) but equally, photography also already contains a non-authoring position that Sekula exploits. In Sekula's work, it is both the position of authorship and an empirical relation to history (of documentation, photographic proof) that is bound up in his critique. He is both invested in the photographic image, and employs Conceptualist strategies of exhibition and display to unsettle this image.

Writing on Sekula in view of Marxist theories of abstraction and as a practice that through "dogged and nuanced inquiry" puts pressure on contemporary logistics, theorist Alberto Toscano claims that Sekula's works move "from aesthetic form to social

5   Benjamin H.D. Buchloh discusses Sekula's relationship to Conceptualism's uses of photography in "Allan Sekula: Photography between Discourse and Document," in *Fish Story: Allan Sekula*, 2nd ed. (Düsseldorf: Richter Verlag, 2002), 195.

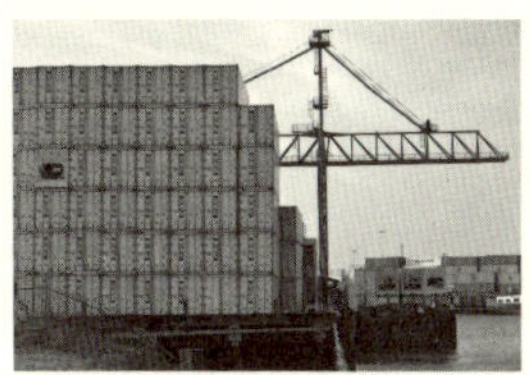

Rotterdam harbor, 2016
(image: Bik Van der Pol)

→ p 177

form."[6] Yet the question of how they complete this movement, "a reduction of phenomena of artistic form to social form,"[7] and I would argue back again, cannot be made manifest in Toscano's account because it focuses solely on Sekula's work as a photographic practice. Specifically, Toscano's account situated Sekula's use of photography on the one hand, and his writing on the other. How Sekula himself conceived of the "conceptual tools" with which he furnished his photographs must be investigated to arrive at the container—and ultimately, the critique of logistics that Toscano elicits but does not flesh out.[8]

I draw on the art historian Benjamin Buchloh's account of Sekula's work in order to illustrate how art historical canonization functions to limit political horizons offered by the reinterpretation of artistic genre—in this case Buchloh forecloses the possibilities of employing Conceptualism as a rubric for Sekula's practice. In *Fish Story* Buchloh discusses the importance of the "hierarchy of photography" as important to Sekula's work, specifically that Sekula's mining of documentary photography was in opposition to the "apex" of "high art" photography being institutionalized at that time.[9] I am sidestepping the question of the institutional status of photography today given that we are in the midst of one of Sekula's institutionalizations, thus "marginalization" of him or of documentary photo-

6   Alberto Toscano, "Photography Against the Flow: Abstraction and Logistics in Allan Sekula's Writings," in *Allan Sekula: Ship of Fools / The Dockers' Museum*, ed. Hilde van Gelder (Leuven: Leuven University Press: 2015), 47.

7   Ibid.

8   Ibid, 46.

9   Buchloh, "Allan Sekula," 190.

graphy is a less pertinent discussion. I forgo this in favor of focusing on Sekula's relation to Conceptualism, as the operation of which in its historic forms (in the 1960s and 1970s) functioned to erode the distinction between art and "the document" as it existed in legal or administrative contexts.[10] This destabilization between "primary material" and artistic practice in Sekula's work is where I argue the shipping container becomes form.

This betrays my own investment as a writer on socially engaged art (SEA), where conceiving of Conceptualism's document as a root becomes important as this form of art is institutionalized—what I mean by this is that in Sekula's case photography was the "base" or non-art element in the institution, placed within a Conceptual mode of display in order to become legible as art (rather than social documentary, for example). Today I would argue that certain participatory elements of SEA constitute this "base" element, similarly exhibited through the use of Conceptualism's protocols. Specifically for Buchloh, it is Sekula's use of "base" photographic modes ("documentary photography" and "historical narrative") that constituted the political thrust of his work.[11] Conceptualist uses of photography by contrast are closed to the concept of "intervention and change" in Buchloh's account. This political gatekeeping of Conceptualism is telling. Buchloh locates all of the political capability of Sekula's practice as resident in his use of photography (or at the most, as part of a "dialectical movement" between Conceptualism and photography, where the social content of the work is still what furnishes

10 If we, for example, accept Seth Sieglaub's production of the "Artists' Rights and Transfers Agreement" as in part a product of Conceptualism, this was a document that functioned to provide artists with new legal and economic jurisdiction over their work, collapsing distinction between the document as artistic and legal form.

11 Buchloh, "Allan Sekula," 190.

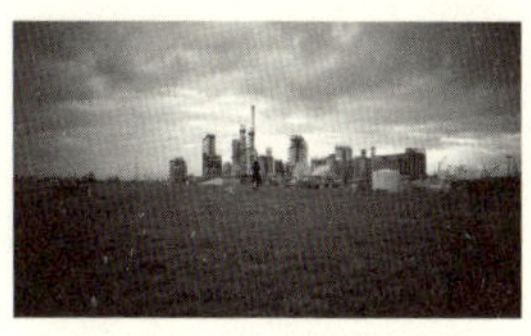

Antwerp harbor (Photo: Julia Kul)

→ p 178

its politics) because the institutional function of the essay (art history) is dependent on such **stratifications**, and on the maintenance of previously determined genres. In Sekula's last work, photography arguably begins to fade: social practice, the "base" element of today, appears in his last work, in the collection of objects that makes up the *Dockers' Museum*. With *Dockers' Museum*, it is **Conceptual strategies**, rather than photography, that are carried over.

My situating of Sekula is meant as a way of **rethinking** artistic precedent out of the bounds of art history's reliance on biography, as well as the discipline's tendency to foreclose the political potential of form. I am not talking here about Sekula the person but am foregrounding the conditions of precedence. We can imagine here preceding "figure" to be like a law, not biographical personhood but discursive personhood, outside of art history's biography and its attribution of Sekula with internal vision or "artisanal skills"—something he surely rejected.[12] To take his practice as precedent, it represents one that relentlessly connected the capabilities of artistic Conceptualism to the project of historical materialism, to the critique of (and in *Ship of Fools* for example, resistance against) the **social relations** of production. Sekula is then a figure for whom Conceptualism functioned as a method of representing these conditions—of labor and of the movement of goods—in opposition to empiricism and as a problemitization of systems of representation which are themselves produced and secured by the same order the work itself seeks to address. This is the ongoing promise of Conceptualism, despite the reification of its canonical forms in the market and the "institution of art." It offers the set of practices that allow for the movement between "aesthetic and social form" that Toscano analyses without specific referent within the work itself.

12   Ibid., 196.

Part II: Reading

We begin the reading now, with the container in mind as it has been made available by Sekula's practice, as that practice is brought to us by the institution we sit in now. To turn to Easterling's container, she situates it as the cellular form that makes up "the logistics city":

The now familiar container, filled with flip flops, panties, animals, tangerines, and microelectronics is the germ of a surprisingly excessive urbanism.[13]

The seed form, we could say, of the logistics city; or the base form. For an image of the "excessive urbanism" that the container constructs:

13 Easterling, *Enduring Innocence*, 99.

The world's top ports—Hong Kong, Singapore, Pusan, Kaohsiung, Rotterdam, Shanghai, Los Angeles, Long Beach, Hamburg, and Antwerp—continue to vie for top rank. [...] Megaships that populate these ports have, in recent years, gone from carrying 6,500 TEUs (twenty foot equivalent units, *or the equivalent of a 20 foot by 8 foot by 8.5 foot container*) to carrying 9,000. As they increase in capacity (some are over one thousand feet long) they must also be unloaded even more quickly.[14]

Easterling discusses the development of "spatial products," like the container or historically the elevator, as illustrative of the role of architecture and design in the facilitation of capitalism. In one passage, she links the radical architectural productions of Cedric Price, whose moving walls and constantly adaptable spaces were never built, to the mobile space of the port

14   Ibid., emphasis mine.

and distribution park.[15] The work Easterling does here is precisely to connect avant-garde production to the most fantastical environments of late capital. This further establishes the container—that which ultimately makes environments like Price's possible—as a formal achievement, with a vexed relation to architectural practice. Thus, the material relation between container and architecture that she plots is another way of conceiving of the shared consequences of form. That the container is like and also unlike architecture: in the case of Price, the container was not yet imagined, but ultimately completes the desires of his work. We might read here that even in aesthetic practice that is critical of the "field of logistics" as Easterling would say, there is also a smoothness or ease of exchange with capital's facilitative forms.

15   "Architectural proposals for kinetic or robotic environments resonate with automated logistics as well. Still, park landscapes are quite different from, for instance, Archigram's portable bots (e.g. Logplug, Rokplug, and Cushicle) that would provide individual mediated environments in a wilderness. Nor are AGVs analogous to the gizmos of Reyner Banham's fascinations: the gun, portable motor, or other devices to be slung over the shoulder and used to format a new territory. The park's automatic warehouses do resemble some of Cedric Price's proposals for the Portteries Thinkbelt, Phun City, or the Twenty Four Hour Economic Toy. Price imagined universities, performance spaces, and houses with traveling programs and scheduled responses to the inhabitant's wishes, so that one's classroom or office could simply arrive by gantry at the desired moment. In these constructions, just as in the warehouses, the object of transport is not a passenger but the building itself." Easterling, *Enduring Innocence*, 110.

On the relation of Conceptualism to the automation of logistics, Easterling charts the correspondence between system and manifestation. System and manifestation was central to the operation of mid-century Conceptualism. Easterling lays out this relation as key to the work of the port (or here, its non-maritime equivalent, the distribution park): "*Whatever the flicker of media persuasion or the instant transfers of virtual wealth, parks are the materializations of digital capital that reside on the network side of the computer screen.*"[16]

There is a system and the material manifestation of that system, which cannot be traced back to a single "hand." Of course, art is attributed to a single hand, and this is how it circulates and accrues value, but Conceptualism's desire is to remove authorship—to manifest a system independently of individual maker—just as it "de-skills" or removes labor from artistic production. Sekula documents this removal of labor in the port and park as the suppression and firing of its individual workers.

While historically Conceptualism's distanciation of authorship through processes of "de-skilling" constituted a politically resistant model of practice in art of the mid-century, it is also aligned with the "de-skilling" (erosion of manual labor) and automation of port management in the logistics city. Both (de-skilling in art and its twin in the port) occur roughly within the periodization of neoliberalism (1970s to today). In the context of the port, Easterling illustrates how this eradicates political accountability. The automation of management and its correspondent disintegration of political liability in logistics cities composes their autonomous status outside of national and international law. Conceptualism cannot simply comment on this autonomy as it is, in part, formally imbricated with it.

With Harney and Moten, we see how automation can be read further. Not only as in proximity to the loss of authorship in the story of Conceptualism, or as

16   Ibid., 99–100, emphasis mine.

a process enabling management to overtake political or ethical accountability. They trace it back further, to a process forged against the subject:

> Where did logistics get this ambition to connect bodies, objects, affects, information, without subjects, without the formality of subjects, as if it could reign sovereign over the informal, the concrete and generative indeterminacy of material life? The truth is, modern logistics was born that way. Or more precisely it was born in resistance to, given as the acquisition of, this ambition, this desire and this practice of the informal. Modern logistics is founded with the first great movement of commodities, the ones that could speak. It was founded in the Atlantic slave trade, founded against the Atlantic slave. Breaking from the plundering accumulation of armies to the primitive accumulation of capital, modern logistics was marked, branded, seared with the transportation of the commodity labor that was not, and ever after would not be, no matter who was in

that hold or *containerized* in that ship. From the motley crew who followed in the red wakes of these slave ships, to the prisoners shipped to the settler colonies, to the mass migrations of industrialisation in the Americas, to the indentured slaves from India, China, and Java, to the trucks and boats leading north across the Mediterranean or the Rio Grande, to one way tickets from the Philippines to the Gulf States or Bangladesh to Singapore, logistics was always the transport of slavery, not "free" labor. Logistics remains, as ever, the transport of objects that is held in the movement of things. And the transport of things remains, as ever, logistics' unrealizable ambition.[17]

Thus, as we sit in proximity to the port of Antwerp, we cannot only picture its current laborers, or Sekula's workmen. Rather than a narrative by which the subject is eradicated by automation, what of those whose negation birthed modern logistics? This movement "without the formality of subjects"— logistics—that Sekula seeks to record, cannot be represented in the space he occupies. His focus on the container is one such knowing lack:

17   Harney and Moten, *The Undercommons*, 92.

What of those who were not just labor but commodity, not just in production but in circulation, not just in circulation but in distribution as property, not just property but property that reproduced and realized itself? The standpoint of no standpoint, everywhere and nowhere, of never and to come, of thing and nothing. If the proletariat was thought capable of blowing the foundations sky high, what of the shipped, what of the containerized? What could such flesh do? Logistics somehow knows that it is not true that we do not yet know what flesh can do. There is a social capacity to instantiate again and again the exhaustion of the standpoint as undercommon ground that logistics knows as unknowable, calculates as an absence that it cannot have but always longs for, that it cannot, but longs, to be or, at least, to be around, to surround. Logistics senses this capacity as never before—this historical insurgent legacy, this

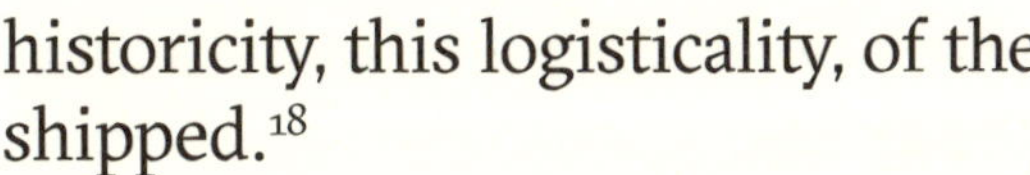

historicity, this logisticality, of the shipped.[18]

What of the containerized? If Sekula's practice is read through photography, this misses the more cutting absent-presence of the containerized that the larger operation of his practice entails. The use of Conceptual mechanisms, that which deny revelation, which are empty frames and disconnected fragments of text, which display its integral automation, speak of the photographs as futile and of itself as a process that begins to get at uninhabited movement. Sekula's practice "calculates as an absence that it cannot have but always longs for." In the same gesture, it refuses the "surrounding" that representation inevitably brings.

As an ending, in both Easterling and Harney and Moten's texts, the sea appears as a rogue element. Both are fixated on how it allows for and forecloses fluid passage of logistical movement. Easterling has an entire chapter on the sea, processing many theories of it, where she seeks it as a substance in flux in proximity to capital. Turn to it at another moment, for now let us find a preview in the following:

The quarantined territories of ports and parks are, strangely, another iteration of the dream of optimized frictionless passage. Yet, like the maritime metaphors for globalization, they encounter both hard and slushy waters. Whatever their mixtures of

18   Ibid., 93.

greedy heuristics—perfect closure with reciprocity, excess without neuroses, or cheating with absolute control—parks are the likely targets of the very political contingencies they have supposedly banished.[19]

What she means by the first sentence—that such quarantined territories are another version of frictionless passage—is that by quarantining themselves, ports secure unrestricted operation with regard to international regulation. Imaging of the sea as substance facilitates her argument. This perhaps delivers us back to Sekula's photographs and their necessary presentation of the sea. In tandem, Harney and Moten similarly register the sea in relation to substance, from smoothness to obstruction. The sea's fluidity though emerges as resistant, facilitative to zero:

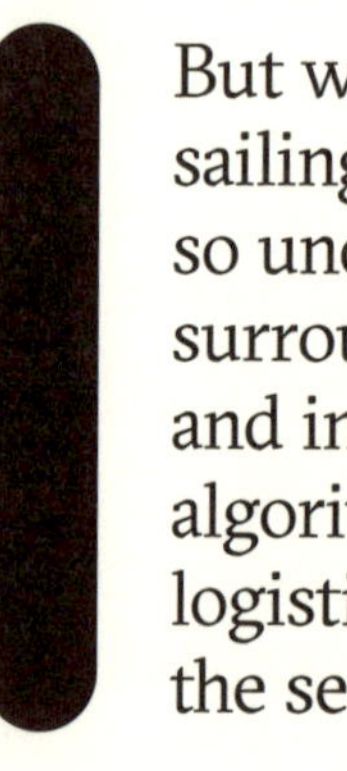

But what might look like smooth sailing, flat waters, flat being, is not so undisturbed. Uncertainty surrounds the holding of things and in a manner [...] in which the algorithm generates it own critique, logistics discovers too late that the sea has no back door.[20]

19   Easterling, *Enduring Innocence*, 118.
20   Harney and Moten, *The Undercommons*, 91.

Sarah Pierce

As If!

87 — 100

To **rebel** is to have a relationship to authority and to call that authority into question. With this **questioning** rebellion begins—before the acts that carry rebellion to other places, before outward refusals or demands, before violence or justice, a shift takes place in the mind, a questioning, without which there is no rebellion. In these earliest stages, rebellion is nothing more than rebellious thought. Without acting rebellion can hover in this place—for years, perhaps forever—holding. And yet, without changing anything, things have changed.

Albert Camus wrote his treatise, *The Rebel*, to address the core of rebellious thought—caught as it were in the gesture of its own beginning and the questioning that calls everything into question ("the whole of creation").[1]

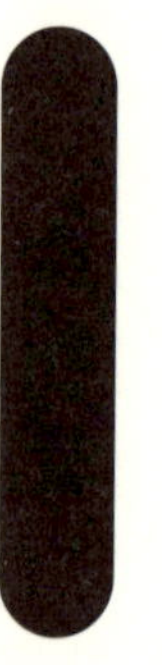

From the moment that the rebel finds his voice—even though he says nothing but "no"—he begins to desire and to judge. The rebel, in the etymological sense, does a complete turnabout. He acted under the lash of his master's whip. Suddenly he turns and faces him.[2]

1   Albert Camus, *The Rebel: An Essay on Man in Revolt* (New York: Vintage, 1991), 16.

2   Ibid., 10.

Every act of rebellion involves a question of justice, a judgment that simultaneously asks: Who are you to judge / who am I? The rebel questions authority, and then turns to face the master. It is a metaphysical, if not structural, shift; the rebel is accountable for what happens next. First questioning, why am I here and you are there? Then turning. And then, facing the master the rebel says, no. No more.

This Is the Limit

In what happens next lies the crucial difference between rebellion and revolution. Revolution proceeds toward violence to subvert and replace, and leaves the question of justice to later, to whomever is left holding the whip—leaving judgment to another realm altogether (to the Ultimate Judge). Master becomes slave; slave becomes the new master. Power remains constant. Rebellion, on the other hand *turns*, and this "turn" (in turn) brings a struggle back to questions that previously appeared settled and resolved, and infuses them with other desires, other judgments. Things have changed, and with them a different subject emerges—a new subject. Irit Rogoff writes, "In a 'turn,' we shift away from something or *toward* or *around* something, and it is *we* who are in movement, rather than *it*. Something is activated in us, perhaps even actualized, as we move."[3] Neither slave nor master, the rebel confronts the order of things, legitimated by the sudden and dazzling perception that a truth has gone unrecognized.

I Rebel—Therefore We Exist

Camus moves through the historical and existential development of rebellion in three parts: 1) The rebellion of the slave whose affirmation, "I rebel, therefore we exist," reveals shared conditions, a simultaneity that places the master *among*, as opposed to *above*; 2) Metaphysical rebellion: "I rebel, therefore we exist. And we are alone." Present struggles win out over a redeemed future, justice comes before action, judgment happens here and now; and 3) Rebellion at grips with history: "I rebel, therefore we exist, we are alone, and justice is a living thing."[4] For Camus, rebellion exists with a "strange form of love," that recognizes all others.[5] A recognition of the Other and oneself as *other*. Justice lives through us.

I rebel—therefore we exist. This turn of phrase transforms the existential singularity of a thinking subject (Descartes) into the "we" of existence—a community *known* through rebellion. The community of rebellion is without authority, without history.

3 Irit Rogoff, "Turning," *e-flux journal*, no. 0 (November 2008), accessed April 1, 2017, http://www.e-flux.com/journal/00/68470/turning/.

4 Camus, *The Rebel*, 219.

5 Ibid., 220.

The community with only a present, for whom living is a radicality, a marked existence, a shared rebellion.

This premise aligns with a way of speaking which necessitates a rethinking of "presence"—of what it means to "be present"—and for the appearance of what typically remains marginal or unseen. The slave *turns* and *faces* the master and, in doing so, performs a limit, enforcing a boundary. The limit is *here*, not there. It is not indeterminate or in-between or unfixed; it is not negotiable. It is deeply preserved by a radical justice. This is the justice of Black Lives Matter, of Standing Rock, of the LA Tenants Union, and every place where a demand for justice speaks from *inside*. These are pivotal moments, where agency (one's power to act) is *staying put*; where declaring action is a refusal to move, to abandon, to withdraw, or become otherwise *unfixed*. Justice administered as a hypothetical "what if..." is not justice. Justice is not a glossing over of real divides or played out through symbolic reassemblies of power. To speak from inside is not necessarily to speak as an insider. It is to risk one's authority and experience, by connecting these directly to the lived experiences of others. To speak from inside is to act *justly* at the moment of rebellion—at the very moment when violence and action are face-to-face. It is to produce *another* inside that is incommensurable with the one that exists; an inside where there is no binary split (us and them / in or out / for or against), no margin and no escape.

Justice after Occupy

In the beginnings of Occupy Wall Street, voices on both the political Left and Right equally admonished that no coherent demands were coming out of the movement. "What do they *want*?" was the exasperated rejoinder (and dismissal) of Occupy's main slogan, "We are the 99%." Meanwhile, Occupy's main action—occupying—set up in resistance to the productive force of capital and the constancy of late capitalism's unrelenting movement (which is also its violence). Occupy opposed by taking hold, and gained momentum partly because so many could identify with the movement without having *to do* anything.

Lenin's famous call to the proletariat in 1901, "What is to be done," addressed a subject primed for revolution. A rhetorical question, it presumed consensus in the answer, and worked to similar unifying effect. The 99 percent knows who "we" is—as such Occupy produced an unprecedented level of organizing, analysis, and action accumulated as *affect*. Its "presence" in the form of temporary encampments and makeshift shelters contained brilliant anti-capitalist symbolism by exceeding the custom of public/private space within the economic-scape of a city. Digging in is an efficacy, a means and an ends. If protest depends on its legibility to an outside, its meaning requires being seen—and when the encampments of Occupy have disappeared, as they have in most cases, what is left? What remains?

In a paper called "So, What Are the Demands?," delivered as part of an online conference in 2012, Judith Butler cautioned against asking the very government that so egregiously misstepped to meet the demands of a movement intent on changing the system.[6] Why ask this government for satisfaction? Why legitimate its power? Why ask this government for *anything*? For Butler, the governing demand for a list of demands signaled regulatory protocols aimed at containing the uncontainable desires of a movement whose power lay in its continual, episodic shifts and disappearances. Why limit Occupy's demands to those reducible to a list when the *real* demand of Occupy is for the impossible, unsystematic demands of *another kind of politics*?

Impossible demands, multiple bodies, multiple interests, many, many desires, and a movement with "several centers." Butler's theory of Occupy—that it is "episodic," where "the target is not known in advance"—asks us to consider a way of operating from inside protest. The "lack" of a demand translates into Occupy's abundance, its spectacle and its divisibility, within the protocols and behaviors that determine the insides and outsides of a movement. This abundance is also where Occupy disappears, moves on, disbands—a movement Butler identifies in the shifting possibilities and impossibilities of the political. An

6   Judith Butler, "So, What Are the Demands?"
(online conference, "Occupy as Form," February 10, 2012):
http://www.e-flux.com/wp-content/uploads/2013/05/7.
-Butler_Demands.pdf.

image that marks Occupy Wall Street's inaugurative call to Zuccotti Park on September 17, 2011, shows a lone female dancer poised atop Wall Street's iconic bronze statue, the Charging Bull. The image, created by Adbusters, the group credited with both initiating and naming the Occupy movement, is easy to decipher, perhaps too easy, down to the questionable "gendering" of the art forms of sculpture (as being male) and dance (as being female) to represent Finance on one side and The Movement on the other. It presents precise imagery in support of its underlying claims against capital, while relying heavily on the language of capital to prepare its message (down to the inclusion of the logo *#occupy*.) The "counter-advertisement" prepares us to remain in capital, to buy in to a movement by absorbing the message.

Missing Studies

The political binds us to territories (both real and imaginary) that are difficult to escape—difficult, and perhaps impossible. This is the "promise of politics," evoked by Hannah Arendt.[7] A promise that is not predicated on mastering the political or gaining experience in politics, is not limited to speculative thought, but rather is an embodied reality. To promise that the world can change, changes *the conditions of politics*— it changes things. It is a promise that both risks and affirms what is shared between generations as the

---

7   Hannah Arendt, *The Promise of Politics,* ed. Jerome Kohn (New York: Schocken, 2005), 199–200.

need to think and judge and make the conditions of politics anew.

As an artist who teaches, I often wonder how to deliver Arendt's promise to students. I wonder if it is possible to teach in ways that open up the political to new thoughts and new acts—not as the impact or result of teaching, but as a way of risking what it means to teach. How to move (or translate) a political system into an educating one—into education? How to address the present and the many futures implicit in the calling forth or summoning of an educational—or any other—address? An idea that politics are handed from one generation to the next does not account for making new beginnings within the conditions of politics. For Jacques Derrida, speaking from inside means shifting the ground on which one speaks. It means transforming language's relation to discipline and institution, to its inside and its outside. What does it mean to enter a discourse that is destined to break at the moment it gathers and organizes—from the moment it addresses itself to the other?[8] What is at stake?

The apparent openness of invitations that ask us to act "as if" we are working without limits (what Derrida classifies as "disguised recentering"), also serve to convince us that limits are somehow *the problem*. The stakes of entering the university,

8   Jacques Derrida, "Sendoffs," in *Eyes of the University: Right to Philosophy 2* (Stanford, CA: Stanford University Press, 2004), 220–24.

where declaring no topic "off limits" directly relates to an idea of knowledge as a constant, means that progressively *knowing more* involves a continual reconstitution of the outside to the inside. One can know anything, even what is not yet known, but to do so requires the university. This is Derrida's paradox and why being *inside* the academy feels both incredibly permissive and incredibly regulated. A permissive/regulating quality runs through all of its operations, its academics, its administration; its narrative infiltrates formal exchanges of teaching and learning, as well as protocols around campus life. Bard College's rural campus in upstate New York contains several large billboards sited throughout the vast

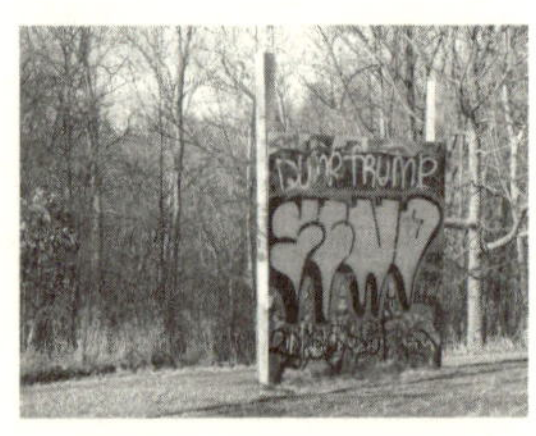

→ p 179

grounds for the students to use for graffiti. These temporary walls prepare us for a rebellion that never really takes place. A gift bestowed to the present student body from the administration that relies on a notion of rebellion as a legitimate acting out. The students reciprocate through sentiments scrawled in neon colors ("Dump Trump," "moveon.org," "Feelin' the Bern") that are, on every level, *well-placed*.

What is at Stake?

What does it mean to shift the ground upon which one speaks—from the outside, the margins, the edges of institutions—and to bring these voices *in*, into the academy, the university, the classroom? The question is not whether what is "missing" should stay missing, unaccounted for, or lost. The question is whether by bringing *ourselves* inside institutions we are doing something radically different to what we set out to do. Our engagements invite us to act "without limits," while at the same time connecting our work to an inside—not just inside the institution, but to an inside that situates, legitimates, and grounds. It is therefore more crucial than ever to raise questions from inside, that is, to raise questions at the level of foundation. Crucial and tricky. Because the thing about foundations is they shift. It is easier to recognize a paradigm so far in the past, so remote and tired, after so much work has happened in its wake, than it is to notice those we are **enacting**, producing, and reproducing every day. We build consensus around questions of what knowledge is or should be, we call upon rebellion as a mode of questioning, but in every rebellion there is something at stake, and this *something* is always structural.

The residue of **consensus** reappears even when we think we are working against it. When we speak about new subjects or name new (missing) categories, we must consider how regimes of legibility, efficacy, and legitimacy capture the limits of rebellion, and the extent to which we internalized these limits in the very spaces where our necessary work takes place. A danger in studying what is missing is that it serves to reinforce what is already there. A function of rebellion that runs alongside this negation is a precise frustration of categories, where not-fitting-in is a kind of refusal or imposition against attributions that reproduce as positives. Where the canon stages the inside (the authored and the authorized) within a paradigm where power continually reconstitutes what is in and what is out, rebellion *holds*. Its legibility reads from *within*, without canon, without authority. In writing, performing, making, studying, and moving the missing into the *unmissing*, what is no longer missed, rebellion attends to those continuities that are with us every day, that cannot be bracketed *for study* because they resist their own codification. Those inhabitations of dissent, that go undocumented because they just continue—as questions or mere questioning. Irreproducible, lost in the document. When we begin to pay attention to what is missed and therefore missing, we realize that far from marking it, it marks *us*. Paying attention has a collateral effect. It changes what remains.

Within this idea of rebellion is an idea of knowledge production as a continual engagement with the institution. Knowledges seep in with Raqs Media Collective, get smuggled over with free thought, migrate through with the School of Missing Studies, or with any number of nonaligned bodies that get in and speak from inside, at the dead center. Not be missed. To go deeper, into the deepest abyss (as Derrida says) beneath the grounds upon which the university bases its foundation, to discover what is there and bring it out. Like a guest who boldly outstays his welcome or wilfully misreads her hosts cue that it is time to move on, these rebellions within the structural conditions of the university get inside and *stay there*—imposing on what is known, messing up the canon, messing around, changing the research and the degree.

A question arises here out of a contradiction. A singular paradox, similar to the one Derrida speaks of in the university, that asks us to act "as if" we are working without limits while we endeavor to circumscribe the limit of what is known. The ever-accruing debt made by the ever-replenishing, ever-present constancy of a (neoliberal) education system, binds our work, binds us, to the misery of what Stefano Harney and Fred Moten call "debt [as] a means of socialisation."[9] We teach with no contract, we give with no pension, we make good on our promises with no guarantees, and from deep inside the university we put our so-called expert knowledge to work. In the depths of the university, our knowledge rebels—knowledge that calls the very destiny of the university into question. Amid articles on Facebook that scold women because they use the word "just" too much in everyday speech, or do not "lean in" enough in professional work, or give too much time because (silly women) they are in it for love, we do all of the above. And more. As the artist Tammy Rae Carland, a.k.a. Mr. Lady, and current

9   Stefano Harney and Fred Moten, "Debt and Study," in *The Undercommons: Fugitive Planning & Black Study* (New York: Minor Compositions, 2013), 61.

provost at the California College of Art says, "If I lean in any further, I will fall on my face."[10]

Speaking from inside means shifting the ground on which one speaks. It is to speak "as if" justice is claimed, not dished out. *As if!* is the irreverent battle cry of those who call authority into question, whose judgement stands in the face of those who judge. *As if!* is the affective disorder of anyone who is in it for love. *As if!* is rebellion's last resort. *As if!* is what is at stake. Do we know how to organize? Hell yeah. We gather every day without resources, in missing studies, in a logic less about uprise and more about the improper grammar of a hanging preposition. The reading groups, the bad performances, the illegitimate works, the mercenaries, the auditors, the prisoners, the regroupings, the protestors, the women—we bring it all in. Rebellion marks the conditions we live out every day—the spaces of politicized knowledge that are separate from and exist prior to political engagement. In the continuous flow that is the university, these spaces remain.

10   Posted by Tammy Rae Carland on her Facebook wall, quoted with permission.

Paulo Tavares

Fragments in Earth Archaeology

101 — 122

Mud

One of the most powerful representations of modern environmental politics is the iconic *Apollo 17* image of the whole Earth known as "Blue Marble." The appearance of the planet as a small, fragile object floating in the middle of the cosmos completely transformed the perception of the Earth, projecting the image of global unity beyond national divisions, cultural differences, and social exclusions. The image conveys a universal politics, but one which implies a process of homogenization of differences and erases the socio-political conflicts that, in fact, tie us together.

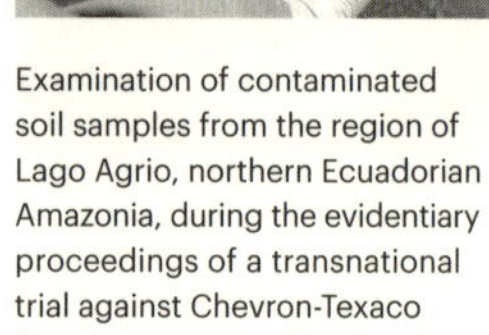

Examination of contaminated soil samples from the region of Lago Agrio, northern Ecuadorian Amazonia, during the evidentiary proceedings of a transnational trial against Chevron-Texaco (image: Lou Dematteis / Redux Pictures)

→ p 180

We can also think about a different image of the Earth as the space of politics: that of the **contaminated** lands of the northern Ecuadorian Amazonia, where corporations have deliberately dumped billions of gallons of crude waste directly into soils and rivers to maximize capital surplus. This black, muddy earth is also a figuration of the global space of the universalist politics of environmentalism and human rights. In contrast to the homogenous "Only One Earth," however, the mud conveys the image of a fractured and disputed territory, sectioned and shaped by power relations and asymmetrical **violence**.

But the mud also depicts a common and bounded earth, one that has been constructed from below by the struggles of those populations who, at the frontiers of colonization, are fighting as much for the protection of nature as for the protection of rights, against both political oppression and environmental destruction. Connecting the universal and the particular by tying engagements on behalf of the global environment with the contingency of local struggles, the mud-earth calls for a radical commonality according to which human and nonhuman rights are mutually constitutive and interdependent (as in the case of the Rights of Nature in Ecuador).

Such frontier conflicts are located simultaneously within and beyond their immediate geography, for they refer to climate change, rampant biodiversity extinction, and widespread toxic pollution. Deeply rooted in local histories of colonial violence as well as within a global terrain of **biopolitical disputes**, they embody an internationalist, universalist cosmopolitics. This politics is not so much a politics on behalf of nature, but a politics for **decolonizing** the very concept of nature and its role in our cultural, political, and legal systems.

Terra Nullius

One possible narrative starts with Brasília, Brazil's modernist capital built from scratch in the hinterland plateaus in the late 1950s. The city's urban shape is defined by two major axes crossing at a central point, imprinting a cross upon the ground. As urbanist Lúcio Costa wrote, Brasília "was born from the primary gesture of one who marks or takes possession of a place, two axes crossing at a right angle, the very sign of the cross."[1]

This is a remarkable description that shows the existence of an intimate, structural link between modernization and colonialism. With Brasília, the colonial concept of *terra nullius* and the modernist concept of *tabula rasa* became synonymous.

The primary gesture of marking and taking possession of a place not only implied the occupation of a foreign territory but it also required a complete transformation of the nature of this territory, includ-

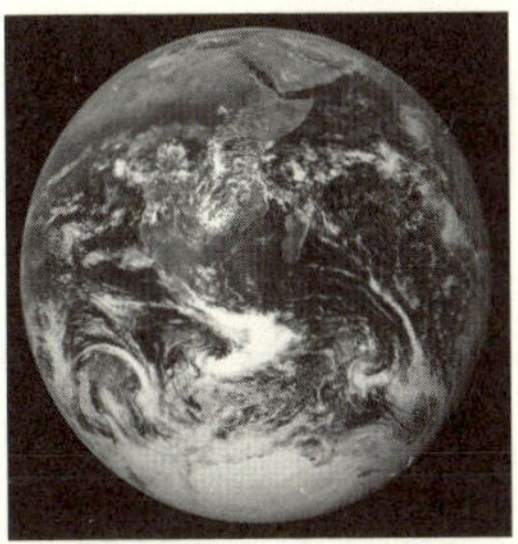

Blue Marble (1972). View of the Earth as seen by the *Apollo 17* crew traveling toward the moon. This translunar coast photograph extends from the Mediterranean Sea area to Antarctica, and is the first time the *Apollo* trajectory made it possible to photograph the south polar ice cap. Although there had been similar images taken before, the 1972 *Blue Marble* image became iconic, and remains the last such image taken by an actual person

→ p 181

1   Lúcio Costa, "Memorial do Plano Piloto de Brasília" (1957), in *Brasília, Cidade que inventei* (Brasília: ArPDF/ CODEPLAN/DePHA, 1991).

ing its topography, environment, and climate. Contrary to the usual perception, Brasília is not formed by a series of modernist buildings laid out on top of a flat terrain. In order to conquer, master, and domesticate the hinterlands, and generate the type of environment that would enable the formation of a modern society, the entire landscape had to be reengineered. The topography was massively modified: vast tracts of the natural vegetation were wiped out; countless trees were planted; and a giant artificial lake was constructed to humidify the atmosphere. The city can be interpreted as the product of a type of "geo-design" in that it aims to fabricate not only a modern society but also an entirely new environment, and through the environment shape and reshape the social.

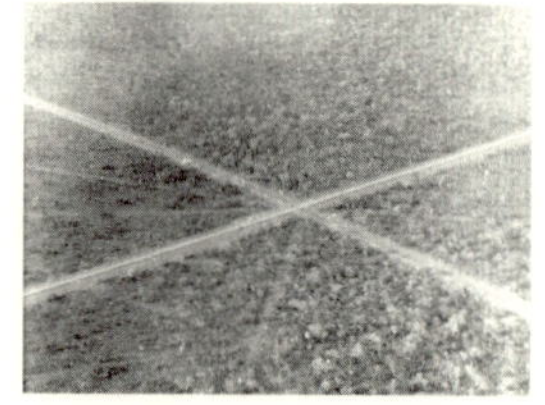

Ground zero of Brasília, circa 1957 (image: Mario Fontenelle, courtesy Archive DF)

→ p 182

Only in the early 1970s when Brazil was under military dictatorship did Brasília become the de facto center of national political power. By that time the colonial project embodied in the modernist design of the city was rapidly expanding toward the depths of Amazonia. Just like their colonial predecessors, modern strategists and planners defined the forest as a void space characterized by chronic lack: demographic emptiness, technological underdevelopment, economic stagnation, and territorial isolation. This neocolonial perspective led the military dictatorship (1964–85) to design a basin-wide strategy to "occupy and integrate" the forests of Amazonia, "a geopolitical manoeuvre to integrate the national territories" in the words of General Golbery, its great strategist.[2]

"Operation Amazonia," as it was initially called, was one of the most significant expressions of the

2   Golbery do Couto e Silva, *Geopolítica do Brasil* (Rio de Janeiro: Livraria J. Olympio, 1967).

national security doctrine as it was applied in Latin America during the Cold War. On the ground this maneuver was translated into a series of radical experiments in spatial planning. This was done as if the extremely diverse and complex social and natural environments of the rainforest could be planned and modified as a whole, a homogenous *terra nullius / tabula rasa* to be rationally occupied, colonized, and reengineered.

Ecocide by Design

The first move in this operation was the establishment of a territorial jurisdiction named "Legal Amazonia," which covered the whole portion of the basin within Brazilian sovereign borders—6o percent of the natural area of Amazonia. By projecting a nearly symmetrical relation between a political space and the natural boundaries of the basin, the operation could conceptualize and deploy planning strategies that encompassed Amazonia as a bio-geographic unit; that is, it enabled design interventions at the point where the "ecological scale" intersected with the "political/legal scale" of Amazonia.

Before Operation Amazonia, most of the forest hinterlands were defined as *terras devolutas*, a form of property inherited from the colonial period which, although belonging to the state, has no defined public use, thus remaining common but available for private appropriation. As roads and development projects opened up these unlegislated areas for colonization, massive deforestation followed. The production of pasturelands turned out to be one of the most effective means used by speculators to claim and secure land titles, engendering a mechanism of "enclosure-by-destruction"

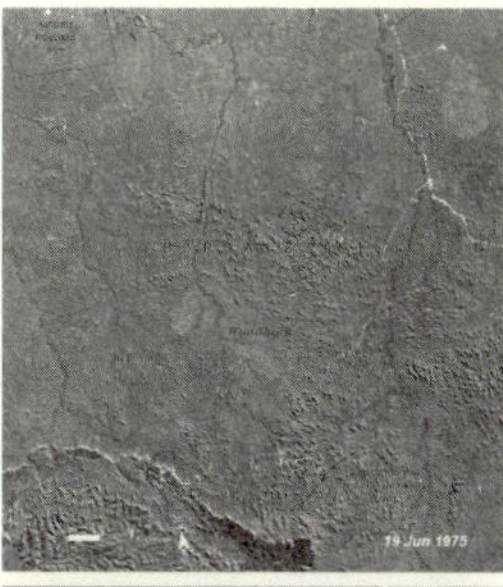
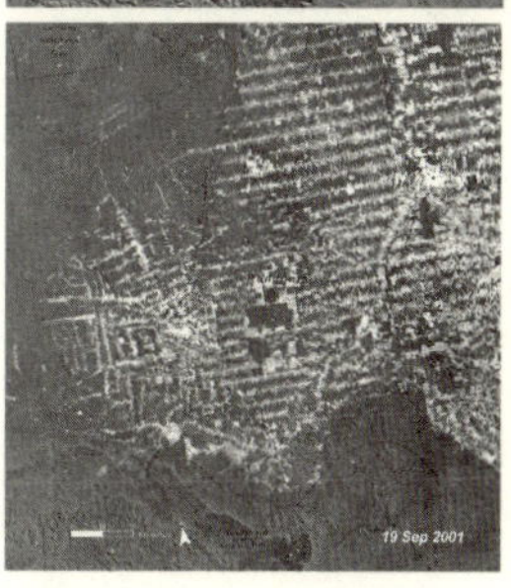

Before and after (1975–2001) satellite images showing patterns of deforestation in the region of the "Development Pole" in the state of Rondônia, southwestern Amazon Basin. Patterns of environmental degradation in Amazonia follow the blueprint elaborated by the military regime and its planning bureaus (courtesy UNDP)

→ p 183

that resulted in a vicious cycle of ecological and social violence that continues today.

Generally interpreted as the product of a chaotic and unregulated process fuelled by a lack of governmental control, patterns of deforestation in Amazonia are in fact the result of centralized planning schemes. Ecocide was produced by design.

Conceptualized and deployed over the basin as a whole, this militarized strategy engendered transformations at the "ecological scale" of Amazonia, which in turn catalyzed changes on the scale of the Earth system. The effects that ensued can be felt in the climate convulsions we experience today across the globe, transformations that are as much natural as social and political. The Anthropocene, indeed, is the product of military coups d'état.

Data

There is an ongoing debate on when the Anthropocene, the era when humanity became a geological force, has started. The most accepted thesis establishes the Industrial Revolution in Europe as the turning point. What we know for sure is that, from the 1950s onward, this process of geological transformation accelerated exponentially. Every index that registers humanity's footprint on the planetary ecosystem (water and energy use; paper and fertilizer consumption; vehicle numbers; levels of international tourism and communications; flows of capital, goods, and people) shows a dramatic increase during the second half of the twentieth century, reaching a stage of take-off somewhere after 1950 and accelerating in the decades that followed. The impacts of this explosion in scale and intensity of anthropogenic interference in the global environment are so unique and radically different from anything else experienced in history that a specific geological periodization called the Great Acceleration—"the most rapid and pervasive shift in the

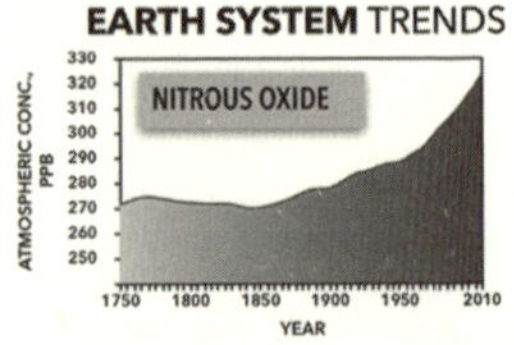

Modernity's footprint on the global environment. The second half of the twentieth century marks the most radical transformation in human-environment relationships ever registered (courtesy IGBP)

→ p 185

human-environment relationship"[3]—has been designated to define the late twentieth century.

This phenomena and its correlative manifestation in global climate change are generally attributed to, and analyzed in relationship with, an evolutionary trajectory in the history of the human species toward higher stages of civilization, technological progress, social development, economic growth, and material well-being. From that perspective, climate change is interpreted as the side effect of modernity; a **collateral** product within an inherently positive movement toward economic and social improvement pursued by humanity as a whole. But, as we know, "there is no document of civilization which is not at the same time a document of **barbarism**."[4]

The data that constitutes the charts of the Great Acceleration and global climate change must be historically contextualized and spatially situated, framed in relation to the uneven geographies of resource distribution and the architectures of power that shaped this new geophysical/geopolitical terrain. In the singular context of Amazonia, environmental **data** must be analyzed in relation to the violent history of colonization of Indigenous lands, particularly under the militarized state that was installed after the 1964 coup. Histories of state

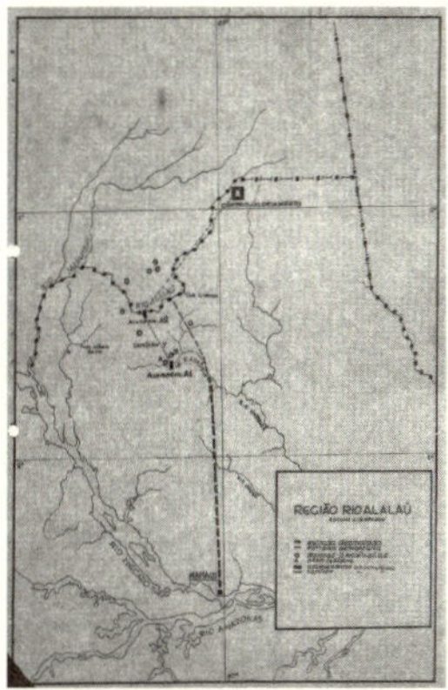

Map of the "project of pacification" elaborated by FUNAI in 1968, showing the strategy to relocate Waimiri-Atroari villages away from the route of the BR-174 highway (courtesy FUNAI)

→ p 184

3   Will Steffen, Paul J. Crutzen, and John R. McNeill, "The Anthropocene: Are Humans Now Overwhelming the Great Forces of Nature?," *Ambio* 36, no. 8 (December 2007).

4   Walter Benjamin, "Theses on the Philosophy of History," in *Illuminations: Essays and Reflections*, ed. Hannah Arendt, trans. Harry Zohn (New York: Schocken, 2007), 256.

terror and histories of ecological ruination must be told in relation to each other and as part of the same tale of power. In other words, political violence is also a "driver" of anthropogenic global climate change.

Territorial Voids

Contrary to the colonial imagination that legitimized the "occupation" of Amazonia, the military was not intervening into an empty space, but in a densely populated and extremely socially diverse "pluri-national" territory. The objective of the so-called geopolitical maneuver was to de-pluri-nationalize this territory, to reengineer and homogenize land and society.

One of the main protagonists in that process was the Service for the Protection of the Indians (SPI), later named the National Indigenous Foundation (FUNAI), a state agency dedicated to contact, pacify, and provide welfare to Indigenous populations. These state agencies reenacted forms of population and territorial control that were developed during colonialism. In particular, they employed a similar strategy of *reductions*, which consisted in concentrating dispersed communities into centralized, state-controlled villages or posts, thereby facilitating their control and the occupation of their lands. By the early 1950s, the entire Brazilian territory was covered by a network of these state-controlled settlements.

After the military coup of 1964, the "politics of pacification" of Indigenous peoples turned into what the Brazilian Truth Commission described as a "politics of erasure." The colonial perception that the forest hinterlands constituted a vast *terra nullius* sparsely populated by primitive tribes was translated into an official state policy designed to generate "territorial voids." Whether de jure or de facto, by law and on the ground, this politics aimed at eliminating the existence of Indigenous peoples, both as a subject of rights and as a distinguished people and culture (ethnocide and ecocide went hand in hand).

Erasure

The Waimiri Atroari Territory, a land rich in mineral deposits and strategically located just a few hundred kilometers north of the capital of Amazonas, Manaus, was designated as a key "pole of development" within the general's strategy to "occupy" Amazonia. In the early 1970s, the government created the "Waimiri-Atroari Attraction Front," a special pacification mission aimed at quickly removing villagers from the zone of influence of the BR-174 highway, the Balbina Hydroelectric Dam, the Taboca Mining fields, and projects of agricultural colonization. By 1984, when Brazil was entering into civilian rule, over 90 percent of the Waimiri-Atroari population had been exterminated. The only 321 survivors had been relocated to three major state-controlled Indigenous posts located at the peripheries of their ancestral territory.

Even with these statistics it is practically impossible to assess, map, and account for the nature and the scale of the violence that was deployed against the Waimiri-Atroari. This is because in the case of the Amerindian populations we cannot rely on evidentiary practices that have traditionally been used to investigate state violence in the "dirty wars" of Latin America.

The most important form of evidence by which these conflicts have been investigated is the identification process of the "missing persons"—los desaparecidos, or the "vanished ones." One of the most common forms of state terror in Latin America was the kidnapping, torture, and disappearance of political activists. Therefore the way state violence is narrated relies much on the identification of the victims by the forensic examination of their bodies.

The identification of the body fundamentally relies on mechanisms of individual personification that are internal to the state, implying a given relationship of citizen–government/individual–nation that the military sought to break and **erase**, but whose existence is invariably registered in the archives of state bureaucracy, leaving an evidentiary trace of documents and statistics. Hence one of the most common representations of missing persons are individual photographs similar to those used in ID cards, passports, and police files, images that denote not only the bodily but also the legal presence of the disappeared as members of a national polity.

Evidence of this kind is virtually nonexistent for the vast majority of Indigenous peoples who went missing. In most of the cases, there is absolutely no record of their condition as Brazilians: no birth certificates, no ID cards, no individual photographs, no documents attesting to the citizen–state/governed-government identification. This is because, from many different aspects, the Indigenous peoples who disappeared were not proper subjects of government, inasmuch as their communities and lands had not yet been completely integrated into the disciplinary and bio-political mechanisms of state control. The state apparatus and its instruments for governing people and land—cartographies, censuses, laws, the police—were virtually nonexistent in the area, and the available sstatistics are scarce, inaccurate, and contradictory. Rather than eliminating citizens from within the social fabric, the violence directed against Indigenous peoples aimed at factoring them, integrating "marginal" populations and territories into the body of the nation by annihilating their modes of life and inhabitation. It was a form of state-making violence.

Because of the lack of these traditional forms of evidence, Indigenous peoples are subjected to another process of disappearance, for they are not considered political victims of the dictatorship, neither do their images appear as part of the iconography of the "missing persons" that shape the political memory ofs Brazil and Latin America at large. The missing Indigenous peoples are "the disappeared of the disappeared," a subtle process of exclusion that in a perverse way accomplishes the politics of erasure devised by the military.

The Missing Villages

One of the few existing pieces of visual evidence of the violence that was perpetrated against the Waimiri-Atroari is the photograph of a burning village taken from an airplane. Departing from this image, in 2012 I initiated a project on the case. The main objective was to identify the ruins of the villages that were erased by the politics of pacification. The rationale was that, inasmuch as the military attacked an entire mode of life, by reading patterns of Indigenous inhabitation in the forest fabric the violence could be mapped and narrated.

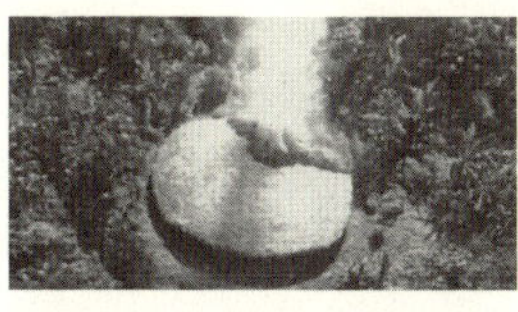

Aerial photograph taken by FUNAI on October 1, 1974 in the region of the Alalaú River, Waimiri Atroari Territory (courtesy FUNAI)

→ p 185

Rigorously geometric, the architecture of the villages was formed by a communal rounded house, situated at the center of a larger ellipsoid plaza surrounded by gardens of fruit and nut trees and fields of swidden agriculture. This basic centripetal cell was highly mobile, as villages were periodically abandoned and moved to other places. Former village sites continued to be visited for several years, since these areas tended to be richer in game species, and fruit trees and medicine plants that grow from natural succession. Archaeological evidence also demonstrates that most likely the new settlement would be located within an area that had been formerly occupied.

How did devastation on such a scale, which in less than ten years decimated 90 percent of the Waimiri-Atroari population and violently dismantled a network of settlements, gardens, swiddens, fallows, and roads, leave no remains, no marks in the terrain? How did numerous villages disappear without any recognizable archaeological signature being left on the ground?

To assume that this extensive and complex territorial infrastructure completely vanished without leaving ruins or any other material evidence is not only counterintuitive and seemingly illogical; it also commits, in another form, the act of erasure on the sociohistorical agency of Indigenous peoples, perpetrating the genocidal politics deployed by the dictatorship by other means.

Botanic Archaeology

In order to overcome this "lack of evidence" we started to look for different modes for reading evidence of villages that had been destroyed or forcibly abandoned during the process of pacification. The assumption was that it was necessary to read the terrain under a different gaze, treating the forest as a material that registers indexes of sociopolitical history. So we started looking at botany, more specifically at botanical evidence, to map this process of destruction using a technique originally developed to map global climate change.

This technology, more precisely a code developed by NASA scientists, allows us to identify and measure what is known as secondary forest, or second-growth forest. Why is it important to distinguish secondary from primary, "natural" forests? Because different types and ages of forests have different botanical compositions, they harbor different types of biomass, and biomass translates into carbon. So if you want to map global climate change and the way that forests store and emit carbon in the atmosphere, then you need to understand the history of the forest itself, that is, the variations in the botanic composition of the forest fabric for each map in time, as well as for the entire global carbon cycle.

The maps we produced appropriate this carbon-mapping methodology to read history and understand patterns of political violence. When you run the code over a satellite image of the Waimiri Atroari Territory, it is possible to identify a series of disturbances in the forest fabric that at first may look like ancient primary formations. There exists a series of bubble-shaped interventions in the botanic structure of the forest, which in a normal satellite image is not visible. These patches of secondary forest dis-

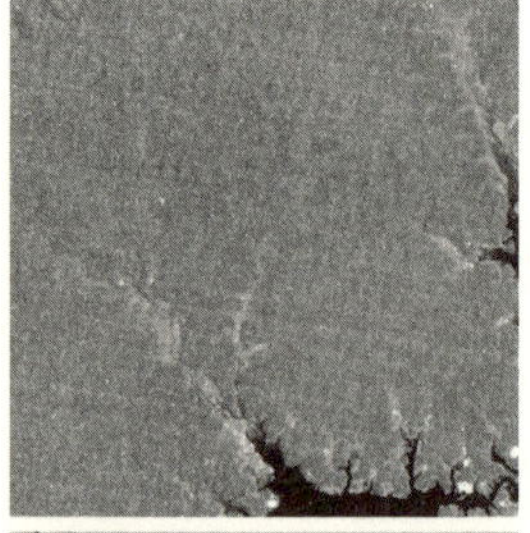
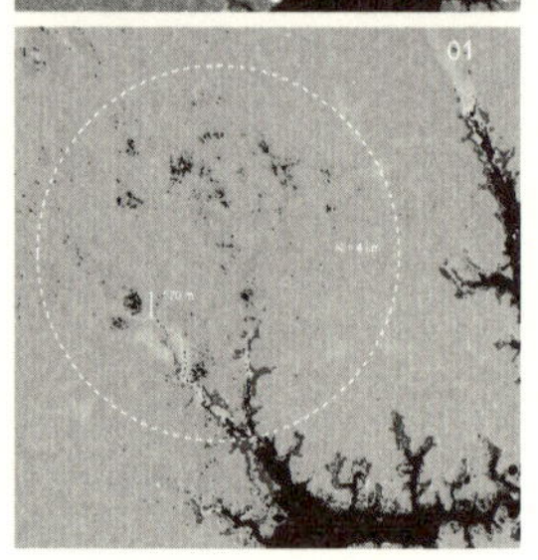

Signature of secondary forest formations indicating former sites of Indigenous villages (maps designed by Paulo Tavares, autonoma.xyz)

→ p 186

play a consistent geographic distribution in relation to the network of river streams, as well as an architectural footprint that is consistent with the archival images of Waimiri-Atroari villages.

Usually we tend to think that Indigenous villages are diminutive constructions that exert no meaningful impact in their environs and cannot sustain larger territorial arrangements. But when you run the code in a vast territorial extension you see that the entire area is dotted with these secondary forest formations, showing that the Waimiri Atroari Territory was formed by a network of clusters of villages organized throughout the river channels.

The **nomadic architecture** of the Waimiri-Atroari settlements with its multiple rings of swiddens, gardens and fallows—the historical movement of occupation and abandonment, forest clearings and regrowth created by villages—left a traceable footprint in the landscape, whose archaeological record can be identified in the botanical structure of the forest. These secondary forest formations, which began to grow in the 1970s when the violence was most intense, indicate the location of villages that were destroyed or forcibly evicted. The visualization of this geography demonstrates the existence of a planned strategy aimed at disrupting, transforming, and annihilating modes of inhabiting the forest that were considered "inimical" to the project of national development.

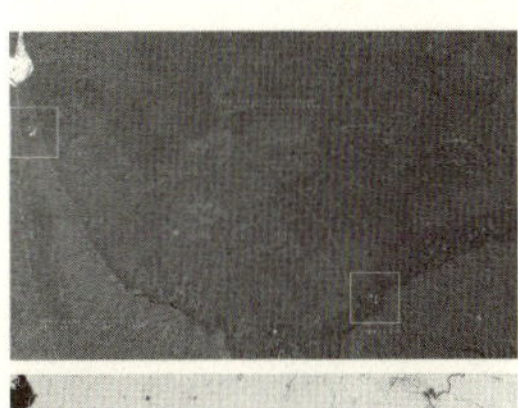
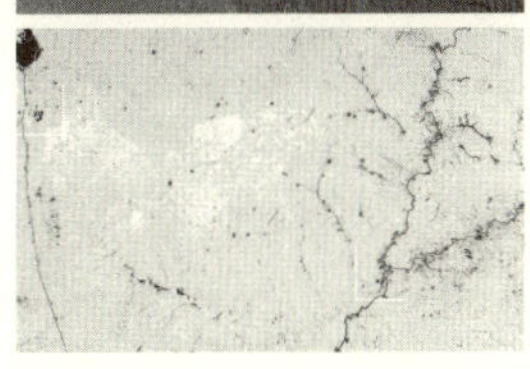

Map of botanic disturbances in the forest fabric identifying sites of former settlements in the Waimiri Atroari territory that were forcibly evicted during the "pacification" campaign implemented by the Brazilian military dictatorship (maps designed by Paulo Tavares, autonoma.xyz)

→ p 187

Living Ruins

This botanic archaeology of the missing villages projects an image of Amazonia that radically opposes the colonial ideology fostered by the military regime, according to which the forest was a depopulated, voided territory. This ideological edifice was inherited from evolutionary descriptions that portrayed Amazonia as a pristine natural environment, inhabited by collectives that were incapable of transforming their surroundings. But instead of a lack of traces of anthropogenic action in the landscape, the maps show signatures of highly **manipulated** environments.

Traditional mapping techniques would give these secondary forests the appearance of a homogenous green mass of vegetation. This **optical blindness** in mapping is to a large extent the spatial correlative of an epistemic myopia that has historically conditioned the ways by which modern science has interpreted the nature of Amazonia. In the most diverse views of knowledge as well as in Western culture's general perception, the assumption was that Indigenous societies of the past and present exerted no influence on the species composition and biological diversity of contemporary Amazonia. But in fact the opposite is true.

Fallow forests originated from Indigenous agroforestry systems "represent a kind of Indigenous re-forestation," as ethnobotanist William Balée argues, "in so far as species richness of high forests is being replaced by an equivalent rich secondary forests through cultural mediation."[5] In other words, Indigenous land-management systems act toward the enhancement rather than the depletion of the forest biodiversity, transforming Amazonia "into an even more complex bio-cultural domain." Hence we tend to see these human artifacts as pristine nature, for to a large extent they are proper "natural forests" in the sense that they may look like natural forests and contain simi-

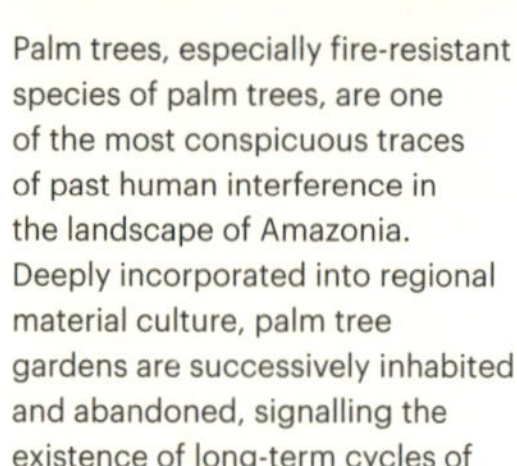

Palm trees, especially fire-resistant species of palm trees, are one of the most conspicuous traces of past human interference in the landscape of Amazonia. Deeply incorporated into regional material culture, palm tree gardens are successively inhabited and abandoned, signalling the existence of long-term cycles of human interference in the forest structure (image: Armin Linke and Giulia Bruno)

→ p 188

5   William Balée, *Cultural Forests of the Amazon: A Historical Ecology of People and Their Landscapes* (Tuscaloosa: University of Alabama Press, 2013), 63.

lar levels of biodiversity. Yet they are the product of long-term social engagement with the environment, anthropogenic-enhanced botanical constructions that harbor "inscriptions, stories and memories in the living vegetation itself."[6]

Despite the lack of other possible forms of evidence, the memory of the Waimiri-Atroari people survive in the living testimony of the forest.

Until the 1970s, descriptions of the nature of Amazonia were dominated by socio-evolutionist theories that portrayed the region as a hostile environment, populated by dispersed and demographically reduced tribes constrained by harsh environmental determinants. Amazonia was seen as a territory whose nature was as luxurious as it was inhospitable to civilization. An important fact supporting those views was the lack of archaeological evidence showing traces of urbanization.

The innovative work of a generation of archaeologists, botanists, and anthropologists has been radically challenging this view. A series of new archaeological findings show that before European colonialism, great territorial expanses of the Amazon Basin were occupied by populous and complex societies that employed advanced spatial technologies to produce large-scale modifications in the layout of the land. The evidence also shows that Indigenous modes of inhabitation, both in the precolonial past and in the modern present, not only leave profound marks in the landscape but also play an essential role in shaping the forest ecology. Vast tracts of forests and savannahs in Amazonia that we perceive as natural are in fact cultural landscapes with a deep human past. The botanical structure and species composition of the Earth's largest biodiversity refuge is to a great extent an "urban heritage" of Indigenous design.

Since they are part of the living structures of the forest, the nature of these ruins is completely different from the traditional idea of a ruin, to the

6   Ibid., 2.

extent that untrained eyes may hardly identify them in the forest landscape, let alone perceive the sophisticated infrastructures, landscape designs, and urbanisms to which they bear witness. Observing, mapping, and understanding this remarkable architecture requires a radical shift in perspective and an exercise in the decolonization of the gaze. Instead of seeing the absence of the city, it is the very concept of the city that has to be widened and transformed. In the same way as we read the city as an historical text produced by social forces coded into material form—layers on top of layers of ruins forming a living social fabric—the forest must be interpreted through the syntax of spatial designs.

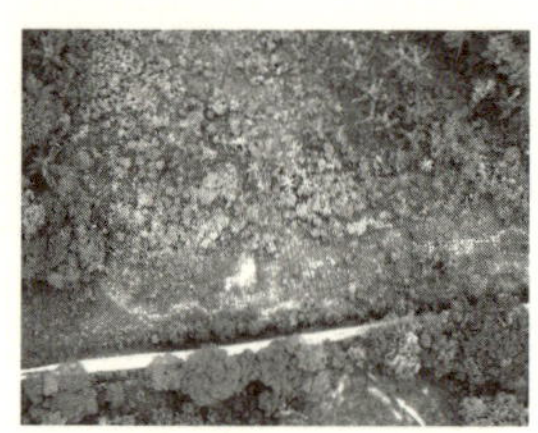

Sculpted landscapes of raised fields punctuate the flooded Savannahs of the French Guiana Coast, northern Amazonia. Nearly invisible from the ground, these large agricultural clusters (ca. 1000 years BP) were uncovered through the multi-channel "photographic-archaeologies" produced by Stéphen Rostain in the 1980s (courtesy Stéphen Rostain)

→ p 189

The spatial distribution of trees and plant species, the geometry of the canopy, the mosaic patterns of forest formations, mild variations in relief and topography, differences in composition of the soil, etc., constitute "architectural records" in their own right. Yet these living ruins are neither fully or exclusively human, nor are they completely natural. Rather, they are the product of long-term and complex interactions between human collectives, environmental forces, and the agency of other species, themselves actors in the historical process of "designing the forest."

Various Indigenous societies not only recognize this constructed nature of the forest, but also extend the boundaries of this cultural milieu to the multitude of nonhuman beings housed by the forest. Therefore for the Makuna, "just like the indians, animals live in communities, in longhouses"; while the Kichwa of Sarayaku contend that the forest is populated by *llaktas*, "villages" or "towns" inhabited by all sorts of beings. The radical *other* that the forest presents is not a completely natural landscape, the absolute negation, or antithesis to the culturally saturated urban environment. It is an altogether different form of architecture itself, which is, in essence, *against* architecture, constantly escaping and refusing to be contained within the geometries of control of modern planning and its inherent colonial logic.

Scorched Lands

Along the southern and eastern edges of the continental Amazon watershed, vast tracts of tropical forests and savannahs are being rapidly converted into scorched fields to open space for industrial cattle ranches and soya plantations. This frontier territory is known as the "Arc of Fire," because during the dry season the entire region is set ablaze by countless spots of fires used to clear the forest. This name also describes the lawless violence that reigns across the deforestation belt, one of Brazil's most violent regions.

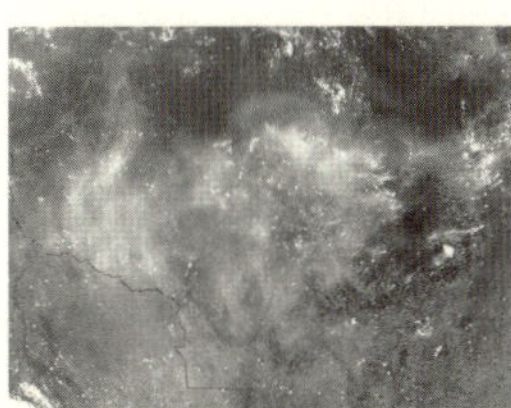

NASA's Terra satellite image captures the "fire season" in the southern regions of the Amazon Basin, a global hub of soy and beef production. Smoke clouds from hundreds of burning sites cover the entire area. At the top right of the image, the vast conserved green area completely engulfed by spots of fire is the Xingu Indigenous Park (courtesy NASA)

→ p 190

Dominated by extensive farmlands, barren fields, and fragmented pockets of depleted forests, the origin of this monumental environmental ruin dates back to the projects of colonization implemented by the Brazilian military dictatorship in the 1970s and 1980s. To transform this region into one of the world's largest hubs of soya production the generals promoted an aggressive program of frontier expansion by leasing immense areas to private colonization companies.

It is in the scorched lands of the Arc of Fire, where massive deforestation and forest degradation have significantly altered the environment, that the impacts of climate change and global warming over the forest ecosystem are being felt most severely, with already some identifiable scientific evidence that this region is set to undergo a process of "desertification." Through a series of increasingly legible feedback loops, this environmental threshold—where the forest is drying and dying—marks another ecological threshold at the scale of the Earth system.

These frontier lands are characterized by a very peculiar spatial economy, which operates according to an expansive and destructive logic that typically starts with the selective logging of the biggest and most commercially valuable trees, followed by the clear-cutting of the thinner vegetation and recurrent burnings. The interactions between logging and fire create a highly fractured and debilitated forest ecosystem composed of much less resilient vegetation, and therefore much more vulnerable to future burnings and further release of carbon stocks into the atmosphere. Forests are transformed into pastures, which are later reengineered into high-tech plantations connected to the geometries of the global market.

We the Refugee

Plantations, as anthropologist Anna Tsing describes, are "machines of replication" devoted to ecological purification and the **production of sameness**. [7] They engender an entire new ecology by extracting living beings from their lifeworlds and transforming them into commodities, simplifying biological processes in order to discipline the unruly diversity of nature into the tailor-made monocultural landscapes of global capitalism.

In this region of Amazonia—the world's largest hub of soya production—plantations are highly controlled environments designed by a combination of informational technologies, computerized agricultural machines, drones equipped with infrared sensors, and satellite-based surveillance. Nearly fully automated and requiring virtually no workforce, these empty, sterile ecologies are sustained by the massive application of chemical fertilizers and pesticides produced by the transnational corporations Monsanto and Syngenta that are popularly known in this region as "poison."

7   Anna L. Tsing, "A Feminist Approach to the Anthropocene: Earth Stalked by Man" (Helen Pond McIntyre '48 Lecture, November 10, 2015, Barnard College, New York): www.vimeo.com/149475243.

This desert landscape is not only lifeless, harboring much less biodiversity than neighboring forestlands; it is also lethal. Apart from being completely contaminated by heavy doses of "poison," the fabrication of the plantation ecology disrupts the lifeworlds of various species, destroying their habitats, and therefore leading to extinction.

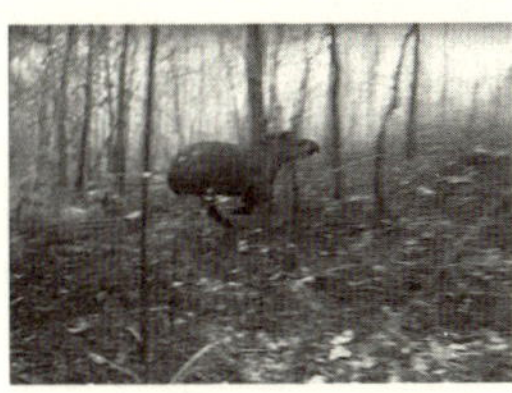

Still image from a documentary on the hunting techniques of the Xavante people produced by the Wederã Media Lab, Pimentel Barbosa Xavante Land, 2016

→ p 191

Consider the lifeworlds of some of the traditional inhabitants of these lands, such as wild boars and tapirs. As forests are cut and burned, lands are fenced, and plantations expand, wild boars and tapirs—like Indigenous peoples—are displaced by the depletion of food and water sources. Removed from their lifeworlds, separated from their ecological means of survival, wild boars and tapirs then turn into refugees in their own lands, and in their desperate quest for new sources of food, they begin to feed on soybean plantations.

"Wild boars and tapirs are a plague," a plantation owner says. "We need to get rid of them because they destroy the crops."[8] These powerful landowners are lobbying the Brazilian National Congress to pass a law that would authorize the indiscriminate killings of wild boars and tapirs, which they contend is necessary to "protect" the global soya economy. In other regions of Amazonia this legislation is already in place.

Here the mass-extinction of nonhuman lifeforms, which according to science is one of the most telling evidences that planet Earth has entered into a human-made catastrophic geological era, is not an unintended fatality. It is the very product of the plantation ecology, being intrinsic to the environmentally destructive colonial logics of capitalist expansion. Extinction is a project, authorized by law and perpetrated by design. The plantation is a biopolitics—a mode of governing life; it is also a necropolitics—a death machinery.

8   Interview with the author.

Such necropolitics not only affect the lifeworlds of wild boars and tapirs, because wild boars and tapirs are not just a collection of individuals: they are networks, they are an entire social ecology. Wild boars and tapirs play an important function in the diet of Indigenous communities, being a primary source of protein, and also occupy a fundamental place in their cosmologies. The Xavante Indigenous peoples with whom we met during the trip told us that wild boars and tapirs are disappearing from this area of Amazonia, either because farmers are killing them, or because they are being poisoned by the soybeans. "They are no longer here," the Xavante say. "Their flesh does not taste the same as before."[9] Fish too are disappearing, and also armadillos, birds, and trees and the entire forest, and together with the forest the multiple lifeworlds sustained by it.

Geopolitics

Tapirs and wild boars occupy a radically different, asymmetrical position within the ecology of the plantation and the ecology of the forest. In the plantation, they are pests, the enemy that needs to be exterminated; in the forest they are the source of life, the companion species that need to be cared for and nurtured. The foundation of such asymmetry is not only ecological and cultural. Above all, it is a political asymmetry that draws a line of conflict between two distinct forms of life and forms of dealing with life, two modes of relating to and producing nature—an "ontological" clash between incommensurable cosmologies.

"Politics is not made up of power relationships," philosopher Jacques Rancière writes, "it is made up of relationships between worlds."[10] In the colonial frontiers of Amazonia this sentence acquires a very concrete, violent dimension, describing a global battle

9   Ibid.

10   Jacques Rancière, *Disagreement* (Minneapolis: University of Minnesota Press, 1999), 42.

which, within the context of a planet ravaged by environmental destruction, climate change, and extinctions, concerns the very the nature of this world, and what the changing nature of this world will be.

Deadly Environment

During the last decade, the colonial frontier's expansionist movement over Amazonia accelerated exponentially, and this process has been accompanied by escalating violence against Indigenous peoples, and land and nature rights defenders. Data collected by the rights advocacy agency Pastoral Land Commission shows that from 2002 to 2013 over 50 percent of the cases of targeted assassinations and extrajudicial executions resulting from land and water conflicts in Brazil were locatedin Amazonia, and that most of the victims were Indigenous peoples.

Amazonia, the most biodiverse region on Earth, is also the world's deadliest territory for the people who are on the frontlines of the conflict to protect the global environment.

Mapped on the terrain, the geography of political violence overlaps with the Arc of Fire, indicating that, in the frontiers of Amazonia, human rights violations and ecological devastation are intimately, indeed structurally, articulated, consisting in entangled dimensions of a violent colonial order that is enhancing climate change. Deforestation itself is a means of exercizing political violence, in the same way that the elimination of local resistance by killing environmental activists helps "clear" the land for enclosures and the advancement of deforestation.

Observing this frontier scenario leads to the conclusion, as repeatedly voiced by Indigenous peoples worldwide, that the protection of Indigenous land rights is one of the most important and effective mechanisms for stopping climate change. This was never so

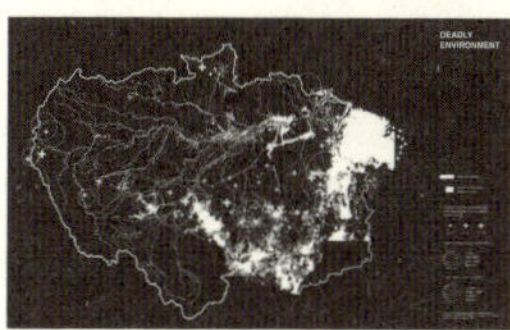
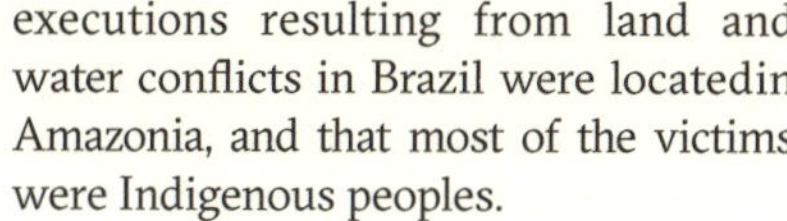

Political assassinations of land rights and nature rights defenders in Amazonia between 2002 and 2013. The geography of political violence overlaps with the region known as the Arc of Fire, where deforestation is massive. Human rights violations and ecological devastation are intimately articulated, consisting in entangled dimensions of a violent political order (courtesy Paulo Tavares)

→ p 191

clearly exposed as in the last moments of the COP21 Climate Change Conference in Paris, when, after the erasure of the clauses that addressed the protection of Indigenous rights from the final agreement, a global coalition of Indigenous nations declared themselves to be "the redline" of climate change. Against the litigation and accounting logic of the summit, the Indigenous movement contended that the threshold of catastrophic climate change was embodied in them and their modes of relating with nature—"we have drawn that line with our bodies against the privatization of nature, to dirty fossil fuels and to climate change"[11]—suggesting that the political battle against climate change is above all an anti-capitalist, decolonial struggle. In the frontiers of climate change, these red lines are marked in the boundaries of ancestral territories and the bodies of Indigenous peoples and the rural poor. In the conflict set between the frontiers of climate change and the red lines of resistance, a dissident political arena emerges, one that is at the same time local and global, located at the convergence of Indigenous anti-colonial struggles and the universal battle against climate change that unites the wretched of the Earth.

This text presents a collection of excerpts from a public lecture by Paulo Tavares, "Over the Ruins of Amazonia," delivered in the context of the exhibition "Forest Law" at BAK, basis voor actuele kunst, Utrecht, on November 23, 2015.

11   Marion Deschamps and Cyril Mychalejko, "World Leaders Signed a 'Death Warrant for the Planet' at COP21," *teleSUR* (December 13, 2015): http://www.telesurtv.net/english /opinion/World-Leaders-Signed -a-Death-Warrant-for-the-Planet-at -COP21-20151213-0010.html.

Nato Thompson

Seeing Power
in Spaces

123 — 138

Moving to Berkeley, California, in the early 1990s made a profound impression on me. I would visit the Long Haul Infoshop, an anarchist bookstore and meeting hall on Shattuck Avenue. What I found there was a space that imagined the world as it could be. Whenever I stepped inside, it was easy to imagine secret communities of infidels who gathered together in hushed corners around the world to plot insurrection. Unafraid of illegality and vice, the anarchist community promised a kind of liberation. They enjoyed music. They had tattoos, piercings, cool shirts, and odd haircuts, and they were unafraid to stand in opposition to the essentials of the American lifestyle. The anarchists, I imagined, were a roguish community living off the grid and making their own world.

My first impressions were not exactly correct—much of what I thought about the shop and about anarchism turned out to be a function of my own projections—but the sense of possibility I felt walking through the doors of Long Haul was important. It got me excited. Much of my excitement stemmed from the fact that the space actually existed. You could visit it. The anarchists had a community.

Adding to my excitement, I had recently moved into a cooperative house called Le Chateau, the name of which was stood in stark contrast to the grimy, anything-goes interior. It had a reputation for being the most political of the cooperatives in Berkeley. Because it was a cooperative, our collective household funds paid for our food, rent, utilities, and, of course, parties. We held weekly meetings—

based on a style of self-governance known as the Rochdale Principles—to discuss the running of the home and to make various political proclamations. In one vote, we seceded from the United States and wrote a letter to the White House declaring that we had done so. In another, we banned couches as part of a war against monogamy. More than **a place to live**, Le Chateau was a place to become. It was a collective "becoming machine" that activated the dreamy parts of my life and fostered tangible—if implausible—methods for making them a reality.

In 1999 I moved to Chicago. I was introduced to an experimental art space called Temporary Services run by a collective that produced participatory and social organizing projects in a small storefront. The artworks, in general, focused more on utopian principles than resistance, and there seemed to be an emphasis on both design and social interaction.

The underlying working method of Temporary Services reminded me of the Berkeley Infoshop. Zines, food, furniture, gardens, friends, and discussion were the building blocks for a sense of home and a community. But in this case, the structure of that form was also being interrogated. It escaped the trappings of an alternative art space and instead created a site where people could come together, talk, and eat. The space operated as a place to produce a new configuration of politics, and interrogated forms of community production.

Sites of Becoming

"Becoming machine" is borrowed from Gilles Deleuze and Félix Guattari's idea of "becoming." The idea of becoming allows us to think of ourselves not as static isolated identities but instead as ever-malleable potentialities. Considering that most of us grow up surrounded by an overbearing culture of advertising, it is critical that we think of ourselves as shifting creatures, so that we can escape the conservative teleology under which we were brought up. None of this is unreasonable—after all, we are clearly capable of being influenced and influencing others and adjusting the inner rhythms of our daily life to altogether radically different modalities.

We can observe cultural capitalism's extraordinary ability to sell us anything and everything—all in service of reinforcing, honing, and shaping a coherent sense of identity. Just as advertising knows that it will win the battle so long as it simply continues to exist, capitalism will continue to shape its subjects as long as its subjects circulate through its system. Better to change the spaces we travel through than to try to change our minds. We are influenced more by the people around us and the spaces we circulate through than we might have ever imagined. Specific sites thus have a profound political power that is currently highly undervalued.

In thinking carefully through these spaces where subjectivities are produced, we can approach political agency in the form of self-production. We can think through the spaces that make our community stronger and more aware of the potentialities of an anti-capitalist existence.

The production of a site of becoming is a collective venture. The sustained engagement with these spaces—and their inherent refutation of the dominant logic of capital—produces a political community. These places not only combine new forms of living, but also activate those who frequent them to produce new models for being in the world.[1]

In an art context, the production of a **social space** is often referred to as an alternative space, but this phrasing is problematic. It suggests that being counter-mainstream is an inherently good thing. In New York City, the phrase "alternative space" implies a nonprofit art structure that lives outside the major power network of the art scene, but most alternative spaces tend to borrow the programming logic of commercial galleries. This method makes sense when the point is to sell the stuff on the wall, but what if the point is to break through these habits and realize something new, something outside of these conventions?

While the language around the politics might feel radical, the underlying spaces that exhibit them are entirely moribund. This can be attributed to the market—high real estate prices require a more commercial approach—but it also points to the impact

1   Examples of sites of becoming are free schools, churches, union halls, collectively run music venues, social centers, coffee shops, barber shops, infoshops, multiuse centers, squats, communes, community gardens, and so on.

that the evisceration of anti-capitalist spaces can have on a collective mindset. People need models to work from and experience. Anti-capitalist spaces of becoming inspire other spaces of becoming. Without them, people adhere to the spaces produced via the logic of capital.

The privatization of cities is giving birth to privatized capitalist form. North of Austin sits a contentious, privatized "lifestyle mall" subsidized by the city's tax dollars, with apartments and luxury retail space. This peculiar merger of public and private aims to remake its inhabitants and visitors. Chain stores like Apple, Barnes & Noble, and Whole Foods (all large corporations who have adopted a progressive veneer) provide civic centers inside their outlets for education and social gathering. You can learn to produce music at the Apple store, hold a class on community gardening at Whole Foods, or a book release party at Barnes & Noble.

Some might argue that this evolution in corporate **spatial production** has injected some breathing room into the capitalist city, which had, until such an innovation, been predisposed against public space. But consider that what has been produced in Austin is a new space of becoming—indeed, a new set of spaces. These civic sites are, in fact, machines for the production of people and consumers. Their intention is education, but of a very particular kind—the kind that creates a new sense of community in line with an overbearing coercive and exploitative capitalist system. These civic centers are produced for the sake of brand loyalty. People who meet in your landscape will shop at your stores.

The larger implication of a privatized civic life is this: it inevitably limits people's ability to discover ways out of the logic of capital. When Starbucks and Barnes & Noble ran rampant through the metropolitan areas of the United States, they did not simply remove small stores; they removed spaces of potential political becoming. Their privatization of space ran roughshod through spaces of alternative subjectivities.

Transversality

While sites of becoming are absolutely important in producing a new kind of political agency, what is also critical are the ground rules of interaction at those sites. For the way we engage with each other over a sustained period can deeply influence our ability to collectively create new forms of being. The term "transversality" can be helpful. I think of transversality through my own experiences at infoshops like the ones in Berkeley and at Temporary Services, sites that allowed for a sustained engagement and active participation, where I was involved in a group-becoming experiment without end—able to throw ourselves into the mix and produce new rules. This experience is what I like to think of as the transversal.

Guattari conceived of transversality as a method for treatment of his patients at the Clinique de La Borde in Cour-Cheverny, France. He wanted to produce a space where liberatory desires and the production of free subjects could both be achieved. Ultimately, he wanted to tie the subjective position of psychology to a larger framework of capitalism and oppression. The clinic may be the site for this, but it is a site always reaching to others beyond it. As opposed to trying to contain desire, Guattari proposed expanding its infinite possibilities.

In considering the way power operates in intimate social settings, we are more able to assess the potential for becoming in a particular venue. This focus on relations and group dynamics is why Guattari is so useful in consideration of collectives and social spaces. When considered in light of info-shops, union halls, churches, student-run housing, and other unusual social spaces, we find a participatory transversal atmosphere where mutual respect, curiosity, and analysis are combined for the purposes of creating a transformative atmosphere. The sites become an ongoing machine that produces a new kind of person.

In 2001, Gerald Raunig applied Guattari's idea of transversality to the blossoming anti-globalization movement. He positioned this framework in relation to the language around "the multitude" that was circulating at this time. He used the term to draw out the forms of organizing that operate via affinity groups, as opposed to the ideological platforms of parties. For Raunig, the transversal is an important method for understanding the ongoing organizationalprinciple of the anti-globalization movement, with its staunch and productive suspicion of hierarchy and its ongoing development of localized forms of becoming. He writes:

> As transversal lines tend to trans-sectorally cross through several fields, they link together social struggles and artistic interventions and theory production and ... This AND is not to be understood as haphazardly stringing together random elements to cover up contradictions, as a political propaganda display of social fields, but rather as a multitude of temporary alliances, as a productive concatenation of what never fits together smoothly, what is constantly in friction and impelled by this friction or caused to evaporate again.[2]

The activist community has developed numerous forms of organizing that account for privilege, gender, and racial hierarchies. Trying to ensure that participants in a group speak with equal time is a method for activists to organize with the function of the transversal in mind. But it is equally important to appreciate the spaces where authority seeps

2   Gerald Raunig, "Transversal Multitudes," European Institute for Progressive Cultural Policies website (September 2002), accessed April 1, 2017, http://eipcp.net/transversal/0303/raunig/en.

in and individual interpretation is given priority. The open-ended query—the avowal of curiosity—can provide a platform for **collective** becoming.

What about the role of social capital in the process of becoming? Social environments where power is in flux, and not a given condition, can make room for open-ended possibilities of self-production. To put it plainly, when it is unclear who holds the power in a room, the room becomes a space where anything is up for grabs. When one feels free and empowered to act, one is able to change. A site that makes room for new ways of being and provides equal space across race, gender, and sexuality can be invigorating. It is for this reason that chain stores ultimately cannot work as a social space; at the end of the day, that space operates according to a system of exploitative logic.

People do have room in their hearts for moments where they are spectators. But self-empowerment—and sites where people can become agents in the production of themselves—requires the production of places where people feel they can collectively explore who they are and who they can be. These are the sites of transversal becoming.

There is a pedagogical equivalent: the **radical pedagogy** of the Brazilian educator Paulo Freire had a massive influence on both art and grassroots activists. His reflexive form of education provided the groundwork for considering social spaces as educational. As opposed to an educator simply distributing his own knowledge to students, Freire proposed that knowledge comes out of a student matching her lived experiences with new ideas, it is something that is experienced and reexperienced. It is a process of becoming that takes into account the actual lived conditions of oppression in their tangible manifestations. Education is a set of tools used to explore the most direct, heartfelt experiences one has. In the same way, transversal sites of becoming provide a collective framework for people to act on their own experiences, make sense of things, try to reframe the world, and explore new possibilities.[3]

Grant Kester has proposed the term "dialogic art" to discuss art projects that forefront communication as their inherent task, with a focus on the community at large as an engaged form of audience involved in corresponding discussions, debates, and encounters. This form of aesthetic production borders on a genre of artistic production in line with performance and civic activism. Kester discusses the pioneering British Conceptual artist Stephen Willats, who took as his point of departure an embrace of the critical importance of the audience in completing a work of art. "An initial observation was that an artwork is completely dependent on its audience. We could almost say viewers are its reason for being, without them it doesn't exist. It is essential for art-

3   All of these approaches stand in opposition to the more traditional ways in which education is acquired: lectures, talks, meetings, and so forth.

ists to realise they are somehow part of society."[4] A major part of Willats' work was the use of the diagram, which would put people into relationship with the social forces around them. Ultimately, Willats has sought out new forms of communication in order to confront the complexities of power and the possibilities of transcending them.

In a similar spirit, the collective 16 Beaver has since 1999 combined an interest in the lived experiences of people on the planet with artistic and activist responses to them. They created a social space for communication. This open-ended platform—and the group's long-term commitment to it—has touched numerous artists and activists. The writer Hakim Bey offered a more temporary approach in his seminal book *Temporary Autonomous Zone*. His call for temporary spaces of self-production and desire gained traction throughout the 1990s and was a critical foundation for Burning Man, the internationally—and peculiarly—popular festival. In *Temporary Autonomous Zone*, creative desire becomes an operating principle for a collective becoming.

In activist circles the term "radicalized" embodies the condition of becoming **provoked**. It describes the moment when people who normally considered the regular channels of governmental

4   Stephen Willats, interview by Emily Pethick, "Art Society Feedback: Steven Willats," *Mousse Magazine*, no. 27 (February/March 2001), accessed April 1, 2017, www.moussemagazine.it/stephen-willats-emily-pethick-2011/.

reform sufficient see the fabric of social life tear before their eyes. It is a moment when they suddenly become aware of the power of collective action and witness a stark contrast between the rhetoric of capitalist democracy and its nascent mechanisms of discipline and control. This has been true of the multiple anti-globalization protests that spread across the globe in the early 2000s, Occupy Wall Street, and the movement around Black Lives Matter. These radicalizing moments—sites of massive becoming of the multitude—have proven critical to the formation of large-scale social movements.

What is most crucial about transversality is that each person gains a sense of agency. Because the dynamics of power are carefully accounted for, ideally, each person who participates is allowed the chance to be an influencer and someone willing to be influenced. Each person works to be the educator and each person, in turn, is educated. Each person speaks and each person listens. Ultimately, sites of transversality allow for a powerful node in a vast network of infrastructures of resonance.

Audience

Every space has limits on who participates and who does not. When sites of becoming have political or proselytizing aspirations, there develops an urge to expand beyond the immediate social environment. How does one expand these conditions? That question can be referred to as a question of audience, and its answer remains elusive, humble, painful, and embarrassing.

Embarrassing because there are no easy answers. When an anarchist space is predominantly white, what is the solution? When a politically radical social space is almost exclusively straight, what are its members supposed to do? How many people is enough? These problems need to be addressed, but they are not easy to solve. Expanding can threaten cohesion and efficacy and complicate the affinities that make a certain group of people work together.

How should one approach an audience that does not yet participate in a given social space? First of all, mutual curiosity is key. A curiosity that extends beyond ideas, and toward individuals: people need to work with people who want to work with them, and communities need to be created by people who want to learn from each other. If transversal mutual curiosity can be achieved, in which people are able to express themselves—as well as appreciate each other's expression—then magic can happen.

Every social scene has its own coded aesthetics, which both produce community and exclude those not familiar with it. This can serve as a defensive form of self-production, but it can also lead to a sort of hermeticism, which has conservative political implications. Finding commonalities is crucial in order to attract curiosity. As we know, certain theoretical languages can be off-putting, as well as certain locations in a city, certain types of music, or certain kinds of art. It is not easy to move across these lines, but being aware of these problems, as well as having a desire to learn, can be extremely helpful in attempting to do so.

The next critical element is urgency. This is even harder to achieve than mutual curiosity. The anti-apartheid activism of the early 1990s would not have gained so much momentum had the injustices not been so transparent. AIDS activism gained momentum by the sheer political imperative: friends and lovers were dying. Gentrification battles gain speed when people lose their homes. A sense of urgency forces people to move past their comfort zones into unfamiliar territory for the political necessities of working with a larger group.

When a crisis ensues, people work together. The scale of political calamity alters the comfortable ground rules we operate by. The most powerful recent example is the emerging Black Lives Matter movement, which erupted after the murders of Michael Brown and Eric Garner by US police and has gone viral across the United States. It is a movement equipped with political urgency.

While these political conditions are certainly a dynamic fulcrum around which to organize, how does one produce a site of becoming where numerous conditions of oppression are addressed simultaneously with the production of radical forms of being? And how does one expand an audience such that it moves across difference?

Audience is the slow growth of a constantly shifting community. The goal is thus to find points of affinity (whether political or artistic) and build from there. As opposed to starting with political topics, shared social forms (for example food, housing, and music) of cultural production that move across social categories may have a potential to build a becoming community.

Transversality and its role in the production of sites of becoming are tangible suggestions for the production of a more effective infrastructure of resonance. The big questions of power and capital will always haunt everything we do, and tackling them can feel like an impossible effort. But the production of sites of becoming that actively try to engage with difference and deploy curiosity as an active principle can be a compelling strategy.

The production of alternative infrastructures can offer physical spaces of engagement over time. They are, in a sense, prolonged encounters of difference and affinity that transpire in the world and between people. Encounters enact a range of transformations that exceed mere words. They are somatic. They are lived. Encounters come with feelings as well as ideas. This is a politics of doing that provides an entirely unique and powerful set of potentialities.

If we consider ideas as space, then we can start working toward ethical spatial production as the first step in producing good ideas. Long-term commitments to physical locations that are able to retain playful ambiguity, contend with power openly inside their own communities, and accommodate forms of cultural expression that transgress racial, gendered, sexual, and class lines are a sure bet for making the world a better, more just home.

This text is adapted from Nato Thompson, "Seeing Power in Spaces," in *Seeing Power: Art and Activism in the 21st Century* (Brooklyn, NY: Melville House Books, 2015).

Eloise Sweetman

Roll On, Roll On, Phenomena (Until You Are No More)

139 — 157

Not Knowing

Is it courageous to say "I don't know" nowadays? What currency does this kind of response have? Often when we hear "I don't know," we look upon the not-knowing one as being lazy, indifferent, uncaring, or stupid. We think we know these people. We might think, "Ah! They can't be bothered," or "Oh! They only care about what affects them," or "Ha! What an idiot." Sometimes we are convinced that we are right, so right that we look down on them with our knowing eyes and with the turning of our backs we might find that our outer layers are becoming hardened, and eventually we are impenetrable beneath our knowingness.

It is true that we do not have time for those who are insensitive or abusive but we can admit that they need to be cared for. Just as we do not have time to abandon people whose lives are trapped between borders or imprisoned in detention centers. We have to care, we are responsible. We do not have time to mess about, we know this, but for some reason we do not know how to come to terms with these crises. Not knowing has a profound and resonating effect that buzzes through the body and can be experienced as fear, despair, or loneliness. How can we continue as we did before knowing what we know now?

How should you respond to that? Which of the thresholds offered by this question would you cross over without fear of being smacked back down? Perhaps your mind turns to the problem of a disintegrating relationship? Maybe you think of the closing of borders to displaced people, or what to do as an active participant of the erosion of the earth and its others. We, in unison, might yell out "I don't know!" not because we are lazy, uncaring, indifferent, or stupid. "I don't know" is not an unconditional position; it is conditioned with, and tied to, responsibility. By this I speak of responsibility as referred to by Donna Haraway[1] and Aitken Roshi[2] who uphold it as being the ability to respond with care.

So then what if we heard "I don't know" not as a declaration of ignorance but rather as an **appeal for intimacy**? Or better yet, what if we began to make this appeal ourselves? This kind of not knowing has a consistency that both slips through the fingers and clings to them at the same time. A not knowing as an appeal for intimacy is one that is deep and profound, actively making space for the unexplainable, the unfathomable, and the messy in a multitude of bodies, shapes, and forms. It is a not knowing that opens up and leaves the door ajar for the difficult encounter. Might community emerge in this way? Could we then start to look at community as a shared togetherness of **not knowing** that breaks apart and reconfigures itself again and again

1   Donna J. Haraway, "Share and Response," in *When Species Meet* (Minneapolis: University of Minnesota Press, 2008), 71.

2   Robert Aitken, "The Mind of Clover," in *The Mind of Clover: Essays in Zen Buddhist Ethics* (New York: North Point Press, 1984), 136.

in an intricate and complex system? How can this be done, how can we reveal ourselves in this way?

We need to hear the *don't know* in a deeply personal and intimate way. I did not hear this enough during my secondary and tertiary education and it took a long time for me to realize that I needed to hear from my teachers and my colleagues that they don't know, and they don't have the answers. This is particularly true for my training in arts management and visual arts, and in my work in all sorts of art organizations and institutions. But it was not until I started teaching that I recognized how important it is to open a space of not knowing. However, it is more than saying I don't know; it is an act. *It is the stepping inside of a space that is created through not knowing together*. This has a lot to do with listening.

Not that long ago I co-convened a week-long political and philosophical arts program where an informal discussion arose about who had the right to speak; those that represented dominant power structures were continually making themselves heard and all others were kept silent. The discussion led to the importance of speaking, but, surprisingly, within the context of the program it did not lead to the right to listen. In a side conversation later, I was shocked to be told that listening was only important to me because I was a woman. This was something I had never thought of before and for some time I was scared that it was true that I was under the misconception that gender programming had nothing to do with the value of listening. For some time I struggled with this possibility but I came to realize that I wholeheartedly defend the value of listening regardless of the implications of a gender bias. Listening is an intimate response to *not knowing*, we as a society do not always have to speak into the void to fill it up. Listening is undervalued, we know this, but somehow we do not know, or we forget.

So how can we listen intimately when it seems impossible? The ecofeminist Deborah Bird Rose tells us through a conversation with Indigenous Australian elder Snowy Kulmilya something that we cannot quite get our head around, but seem to think is obvious:

Humans enhance their intelligence not by stepping out of the system and trying to control it, but by enmeshing themselves ever more knowledgeably into the creature-languages of country. A significant aspect of the knowledge system based in country and made up of many participants is that no one knows everything. Snowy Kulmilya expressed this in his discussion of hunting echidnas. His "I don't know" is fundamental to being a participant in country. To be on the inside is to know that one's knowledge does not encompass all the others; to know that country exceeds the knowing of any given knower or any given type of knower. In contrast to a human-centric understanding of knowledge that would see a lack of human knowledge as an epistemological gap waiting to be filled, in creature communities' knowledge is widely and patchily distributed. There is a multiplicity of perspectives and knowledges, and there is no privileged perspective. Where one persons' or species' knowledge stops, someone else's knowledge picks up the story.[3]

We should not try to fill gaps of knowledge but instead pay attention and listen. In this way, through listening, by staying inside a not knowing we can resist, we can shift into a space of intimacy. A space of resistance that can make space for such intimacy is one brought together through art, the exhibition. Art is this space of not knowing. At its best art has the ability to open up a not knowing that

3   Deborah Bird Rose, "Val Plumwood's Philosophical Animism: Attentive Interactions in the Sentient World," *Environmental Humanities* 3 (2013): 93–109.

does not hold up one form of knowing as superior to others. Within this space not knowing can be bodily, and it can be expressible in different ways than are able to be articulated or explained. Raqs Media Collective writes excellently about the different forms of not knowing that do not place one kind of knowing above another:

> This awareness of how alive we can become is a form of embodied, sensate knowledge, which may or may not be expressible in words and readily available concepts alone. It is what people "know" they experience when they encounter an artwork, even if they are not always able to say what it is that they know. This "non-knowledge" may open a few of the windows that have been closed by ordinary knowledge and so let the rain come in. This process is not only about what people "take away" from a work of art, but also about what they "bring forward" in their experience of it.

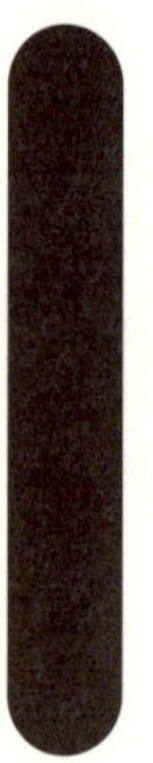 But the artist's "non-knowledge" (echoing, but not necessarily identical to, the public's own "knowing non-knowledge") is not to be confused with ignorance. It is a generative, productive impulse that propels a desire to communicate. It is what brings artists, curators and their public to the same place.[4]

This makes me think of a conversation I was listening in on the other day. The person was talking about giving away your not knowing before you are ready. The person said that a space had to be cultivated and **protected** before she, as an artist, could understand what it is the work is doing. To listen to the work and to stay inside a different way of not knowing she needed a protected space. This made me think of the art organization and how it too needs to protect its not knowing and listen to its work, its exhibitions, its artworks, and audiences. But how can this be done when there is no time, and little money? But am I now beginning to contradict myself? Perhaps the question is how can the audience and the art organization step into not knowing together—both feeding back into each other, shifting between the in-

<hr>

4   Raqs Media Collective, "Wonderful Uncertainty," in *Curating and the Educational Turn*, ed. Paul O'Neill and Mick Wilson (London: Open Editions, 2010), 76–82.

side and outside and always coming back to care and intimacy? And what does intimacy mean to the art organization? By intimacy, I am proposing one that is full and alive and dynamic, it is a matter of scale and a matter of awareness. I am thinking about this along the lines of what Nhat Hanh, a Vietnamese Buddhist teacher who speaks about the self, said: "The self is only made of non-self elements."[5] We can understand this readily when thinking about bodies. The human is made up of a multitude of nonhuman parts and likewise the art organization is also made up **non-organizational** parts, workers, artists, artworks, audiences, and so on. Intimacy is leaving doors ajar to encounters between these parts that might be difficult, messy, and that do not privilege the self. Instead these **intimate** encounters put the companion first through a caring of the body's nonhuman parts and the organization's non-organizational parts. In turn, this care for the companion is also a form of care for the self, and a form of care for the organization. In this way the self can no longer be understood to be alone or independent, as the organization cannot be seen as the sole entity. Neither can be privileged as both are continuously becoming, made up of organic and inorganic forms that regenerate and

5   Thich Nhat Hanh, "Last Talk of the Third Week of the Summer Opening," YouTube video, 1:40:17 minutes, uploaded by "plumvillageonline," July 26, 2013; quoted in Chan Niem Hy, "Insight of No-Self," *Thich Nhat Hanh Dharma Talks* (blog), www.tnhaudio.org/2013/08/05 /insight-of-no-self/.

mutate over time. Intimacy is the interconnected relationship that emerges, flickers, and disappears over and over again; it opens out by *not knowing*, ultimately leaving the door ajar is to grapple with the space that is created by not knowing as an intimate act. To me this speaks to the exhibition that is held within the art organization.

The Door Ajar

"To live in a glass house is a revolutionary virtue, par excellence," writes Walter Benjamin referring to the glasshouse in André Breton's *Nadja*.[6] Benjamin was in Moscow in the late 1920s, staying in a hotel that had its doors always ajar. At first it did not bother him that his fellow hotel guests seemingly forgot their privacy, yet over time as he walked past door upon open door in the hotel hallways, it began to concern him a great deal. Later he found out that staying at the hotel for a congress was a Buddhist sect who had vowed never to occupy a closed room.

Although I do not think that Benjamin might have entirely meant the connection that I am suggesting, the door ajar is incredibly helpful in understanding not knowing as intimacy. As the door ajar can induce encounters based both on trust and risk, it acknowledges that there cannot be trust without

6   Walter Benjamin, "Surrealism: The Last Snapshot of the European Intelligentsia" (1929), Generation Online, accessed September 16, 2016, www.generation-online.org/c/fcsurrealism.htm.

risk, and vice versa. Life is different for those that *choose* to live openly with an awareness that anyone can enter the room. For the monks it certainly was, as on the brink of Soviet suppression it was a threatening time to practice Buddhism, yet they continued to keep their doors open. Benjamin calls it "moral exhibitionism," but for the monks it was a practice based on knowing that trust and risk both rise and fall together; this is radical. This form of openness is very different from organizational transparency; this is laying bare, being vulnerable.

But whose doors am I talking about? This is where it gets complicated, particularly when trust has dropped in value and risk is extremely costly. To complicate things further, the question of who has the right to enter becomes apparent. We know very well that access and openness are not equally accessible for, or valued by, every entity and organism, as much as we would like to discuss targeted audiences and social inclusion. There is a koan in Zen Buddhism that says not knowing is most intimate.[7] This not knowing is called "great doubt" and it enables different ways of thinking or perceiving the self and the world. I take this to mean that a not knowing that is most intimate is one where we are left open and vulnerable in some way. Intimacy is not private; it

---

7 Marc Lesser, "Not Knowing Is Most Intimate," *Marc Lesser website* (March 1, 2010), www.marclesser.net/not-knowing-is-most-intimate/.

is always public as it welcomes all encounters and teachings from those of a blade of grass to an artwork, or bacterial flora in your gut.

At times when searching to fill the gap in knowledge you will find that you do not have the right or the privilege to fill it. For example, I was trying to understand "Welcome to Country" a "practice" performed at all public events in Australia whereby a welcome is given by the traditional custodians of the land. It is a practice intended to open up a dialogue between Australian Indigenous people and settlers as a strategy for reconciliation and decolonization. I met Jenny to learn more about the practice, to ask what it meant to her as a Noongar woman, and to find out how it came about. We spoke about the expectations white Australians have for Indigenous Australians to perform their culture and explicitly share their knowledge without question. What came out of this conversation was that to her "Welcome to Country" imposes the demand of "I don't know, so you should tell me, now" in the most negative sense. "Eloise," Jenny said, "you have the right to ask questions, but you don't have the right to have answers." In this situation, "I don't know" can be linked to how we meet and assess the risk and potentiality of trust; here it is heavy with what makes us up as women and as representations of historical and institutional pain. Not knowing does not mean that an answer will be immediately received, or ever given. But as two persons we did not owe each other anything, and in answering my question she made me realize that through my wish to be sensitive and knowledgeable I was in fact enacting the very same problems that "Welcome to Country" was creating.

Could this not knowing be another way of understanding about "non-knowledge" spoken of by Raqs Media Collective when they say it is not only about what is taken away from a work of art but also what is brought forward in the experience of it. A personal revelation of one's ignorance and insensitivity is not enough. Instead, this is about the way we should interact with one another by coming to terms that they are the selfsame, just as the self is made up non-self elements, which are inseparable. How can we understand this when thinking about public intimacy, care, and responsibility? Particularly when we begin to realize that the door ajar does not mean that you have the right to enter, but rather stand at the threshold and knock. And how can we think of this when encountering plants, chemicals, animals, art, artists, workers, and audiences with the full understanding that they in return may be indifferent to our care?

Haraway puts forward such an idea in the call to consider our companions by respecting them and recognizing our inability to disconnect from the cultural, historical, economical, and ethical implications that bind us to others:

My point is simple: Once again we are in a knot of species co-shaping one another in layers of reciprocating complexity. Response and respect are possible only in those knots, with actual animals and people looking back at each other, sticky with all their muddled histories. Appreciation of the complexity is, of course, invited. But more is required too. Figuring what that more might be is the work of situated companion species. It is a question of cosmopolitics, of learning to be polite in responsible relation to always asymmetrical living and dying, and nurturing and killing.[8]

By putting our companions first by respecting them, and responding with care is similar to manners, which are not about how we appear to act toward one another but it is how we should act toward others. The poet Lisa Robertson reminds us of the basic meaning of **manners**, which are so easily forgotten:

8   Haraway, "Share and Response," 42.

Manners, connecting also to gestures—the ways our bodies meet the world. Many things are better accompanied by manners. Even the largest political events. A reminder—good manners mean that generally you will think of your companion first, before acting. Even if your companion is a tree, and trees, along with dogs, books and the weather, do tend to group among the better companions.[9]

It is about how we enter into the not knowing and respond to it. This is a process through which art becomes incredibly important, as art creates an opening for the organic and inorganic to enter into the call and response of becoming with the world. Like the elements, art has the ability to **permeate** our very being; it is something that we are unable to get away from. It also enables us to participate in the call and response of not knowing. Which brings me to thinking about the work of German artist Charlotte Posenenske that returns every couple of years to remind me of the art organization and its relationship with the audience.

9   Lisa Robertson, annotation to Ian Hamilton Finlay, "Detached Sentences," in *Revolultion: A Reader,* ed. Lisa Robertson and Matthew Stadler (Portland, OR: Publication Studio, 2012), 520: http://a.nnotate.com/php/pdfnotate .php?d=2012-01-21&c=AXmil081.

Her *DW* (1967) series requires shared labor and decision making with the exhibition team, and at times with the audience, to build the work. When constructing the artwork, they are responsible; they not-know together, they care for the work in the open, and they care to take a position. The *DW* series is a work that is infinite and continuously reconfiguring, like a community of not knowing that breaks apart and reassembles itself again and again in intricate and complex ways. As Bird Rose has shown earlier that to not know is "To be on the inside is to know that one's knowledge does not encompass all the other,"[10] Charlotte Posenenske's work encourages the participation of the audience to work with it, to move with it, to negotiate with it, and to relinquish control over it. Here the work asks for trust; to trust the material, the space, and each other.

Posenenske's *Revolving Vane* (1967–68) and *Series E Kleiner Drehflugel* (1967–68) are works that encourage passing through; the doors are always ajar, until someone deliberately closes them. This is similar to the art organization where doors should always be ajar, but where they are so often not. For those that think about the organizational and political behavior of the art organization and the capacity of art to make room for others, this work is thrilling. It is brilliant.

10   Bird Rose, "Val Plumwood's Philosophical Animism": 104.

Posenenske was driven by not knowing to what extent art could change society or even draw attention to its disparities. She took this conviction to the point where she started giving away her work and eventually disappeared from the art world completely, becoming a sociologist. I do not agree that art cannot draw attention to society's inequalities; art's role in the complicated and intricate web of the world is to provide the active space of not knowing, not only can it rehearse different ways of living, but in actual fact it can live and enact them. Disciplines such as Zen Buddhism, anthropology, biology, and physics look to art to deal with the issues that they themselves are unsure how to articulate. They speak about art as being a space to transmit the abstract, the social, the political, or the philosophical to a wider audience; toward a public. Looking to Australian ecofeminist Val Plumwood for a way in, Bird Rose writes:

> [Val] called for a philosophy to […] "converge with much of poetry and literature" because poetry and literature have better methods for "making room" for understanding the vivid presence of mindful life on earth. The quest for poetic forms of writing articulates her understanding that inside a world of dynamic inter-action, knowledge arises through participation; to

"make room" for others, one needs to do more than represent. Somehow, one needs to vivify, to leap across imaginative realms, to connect, to empathise, to be addressed and to be brought into gratitude.[11]

Art is powerful. Moreover, art organizations should not strive to always fill the gap of not knowing, as exhibitions are this gap. Art eases us into coming to terms with not knowing through a becoming with the world, in an intimate and vulnerable way. More than this, however, it shows us that we are continually breaking apart and continuously reconfiguring like Posenenske's work. In this recurrent becoming with the world, with our elemental bodies, we may eventually be able to recognize that the world does not begin and end with humans getting accustomed to an intimate community as a theoretical exercise, but to understand that our intimate community is being *of* the world. In the complicated and intricate web of the world the role of art, and in turn the exhibition's and the organization's, is to be the space of not knowing; our role is to be here in a myriad of possible ways of living, of caring, of being angry, of making space for the whole sweep of others and entities. We need to stay inside the gap of not knowing as a form of resistance to the impenetrable

11   Ibid.: 93–109.

shell of knowing, to shift power through intimacy, and we need the courage to stay inside it as long as it is possible.

Index of Images

161 —— 191

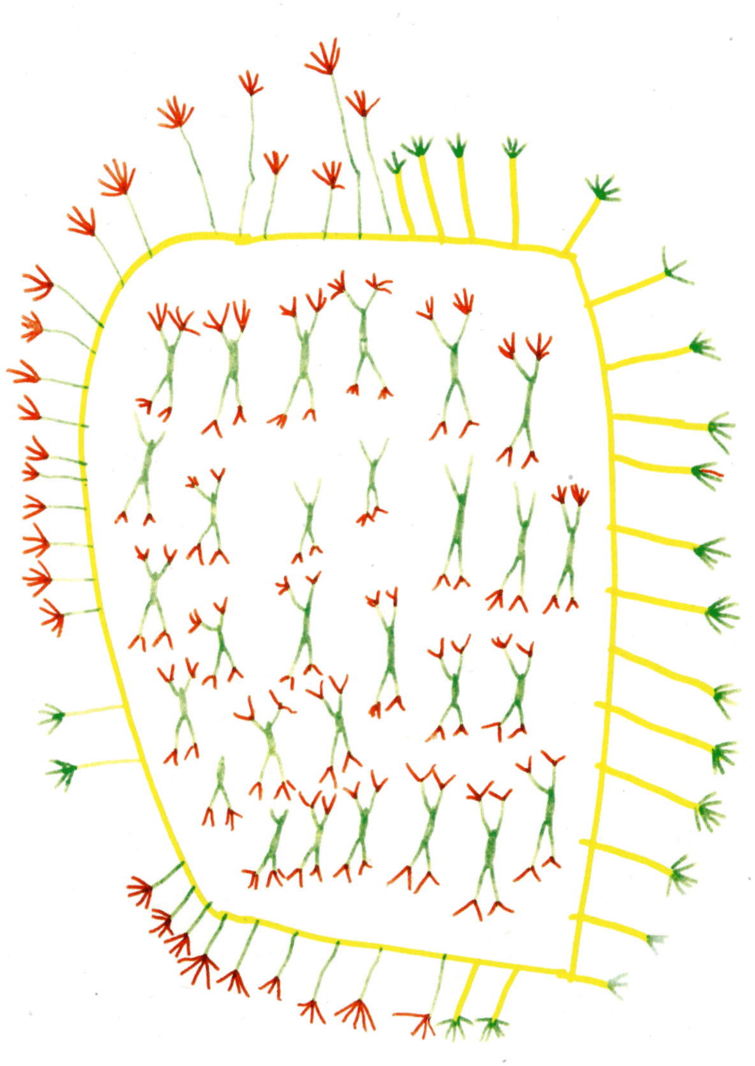

Orlando, *The home of spirits – Hekurap*

p 54 →

Laymert Garcia dos Santos

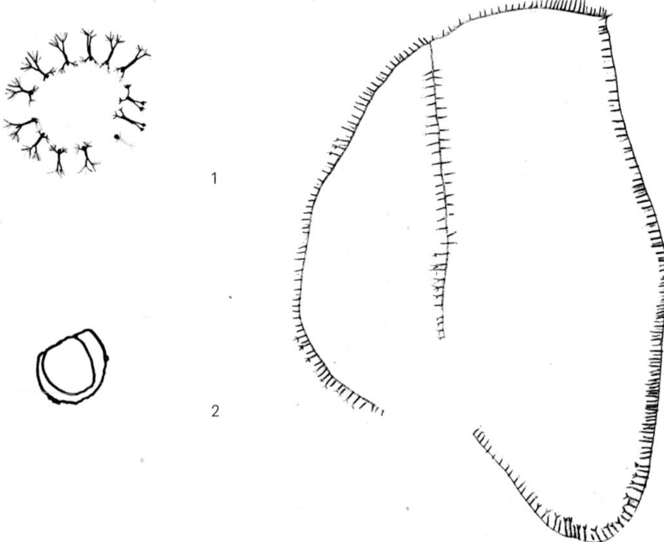

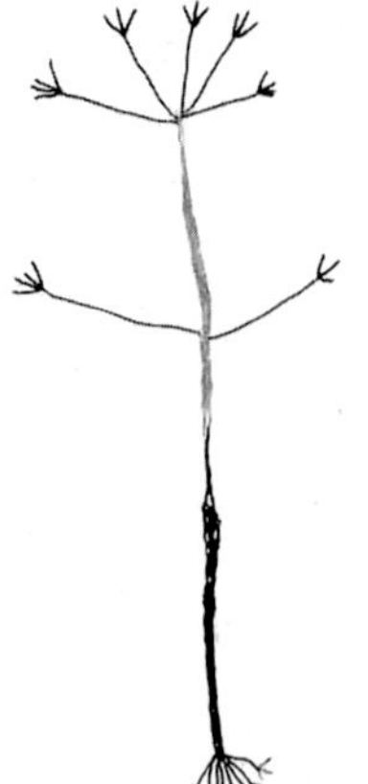

Orlando

1 Shaman Yanomami – *Xapuri ñanomami*
2 Dish – *Mahe a*
3 Powder of the Kurare – *Ñakona uxip*
4 Path of the spirits of shamans –
  Hekura xapuriño
5 Tree of the Kurare – *Ñakonahi*

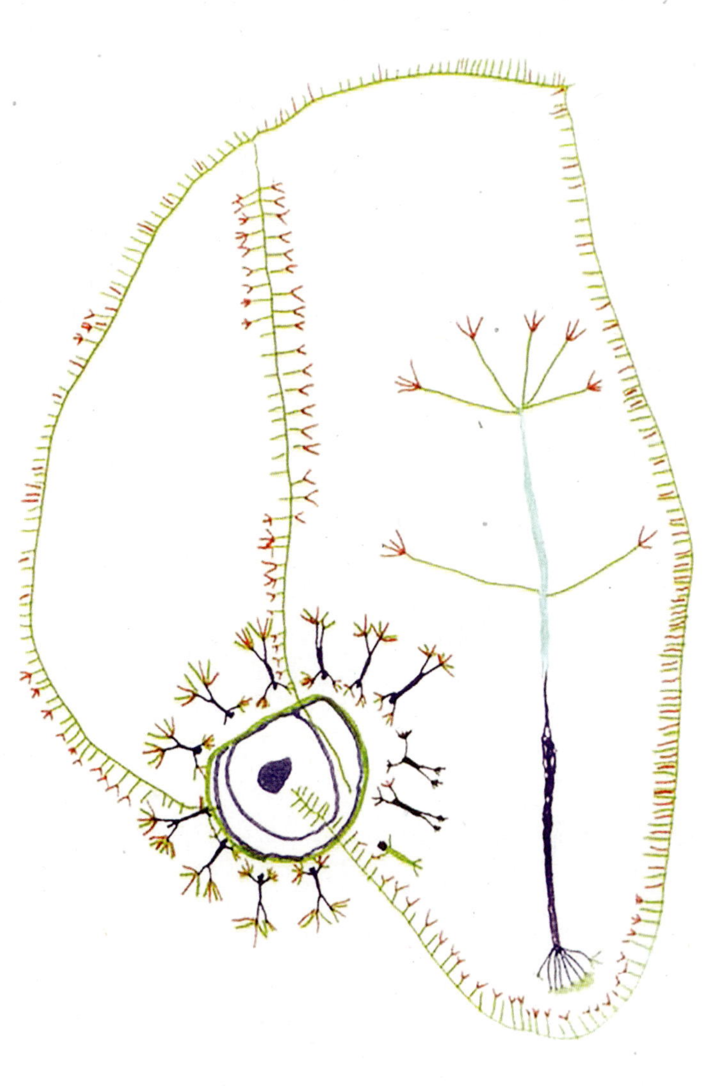

Projections of the Forest-Land: The Yanomami Image-Drawing

p 55 →

Laymert Garcia dos Santos

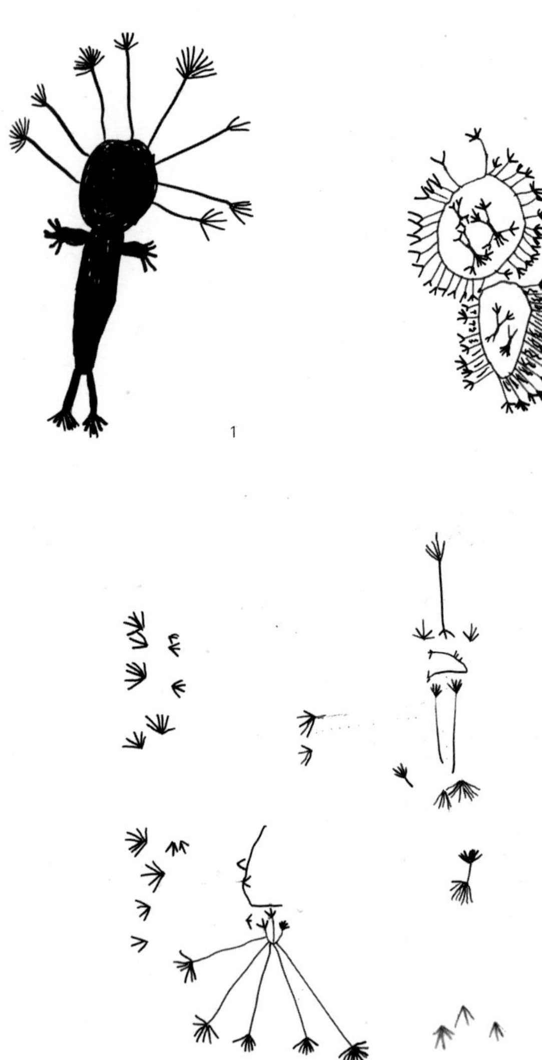

Orlando, *The home of the spirits*

1   The moon – *Poripo*
2   The home of the spirits
3   Xapiris and paths

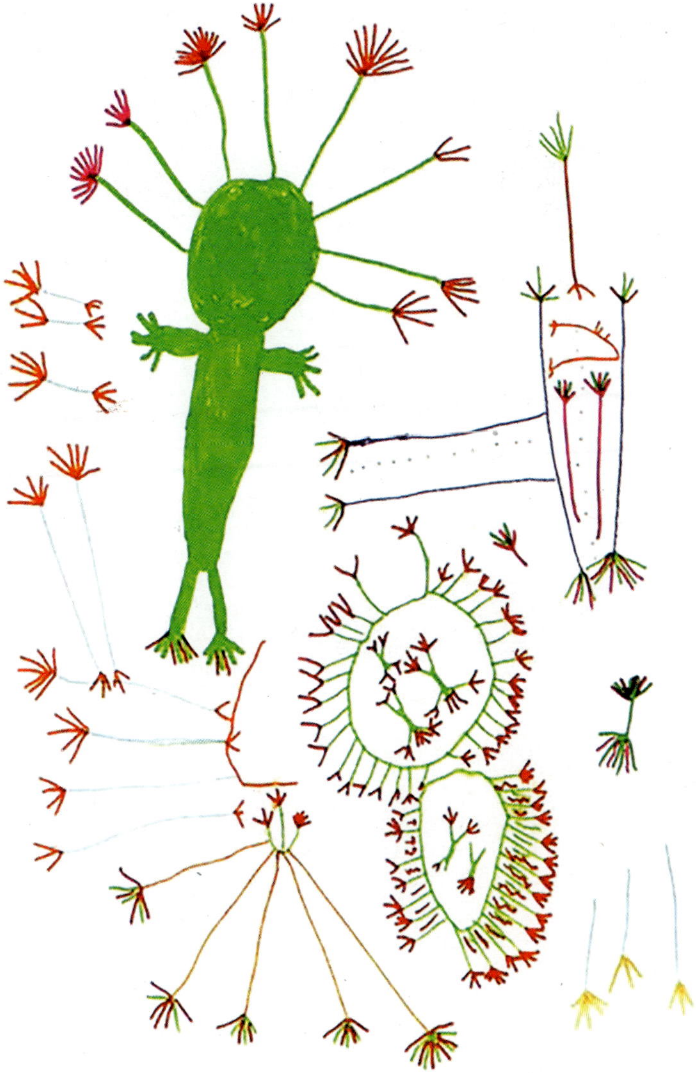

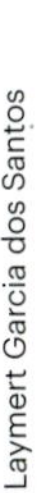

Titi, *The night*

1   The night in the middle – *ñoro*
2   The night in the beginning – *weya*
3   The very dark night – *pata*
4   The night is born (shortly after sunset)
5   The night's wife eats sons
6   The sons
7   The young daughters of the night

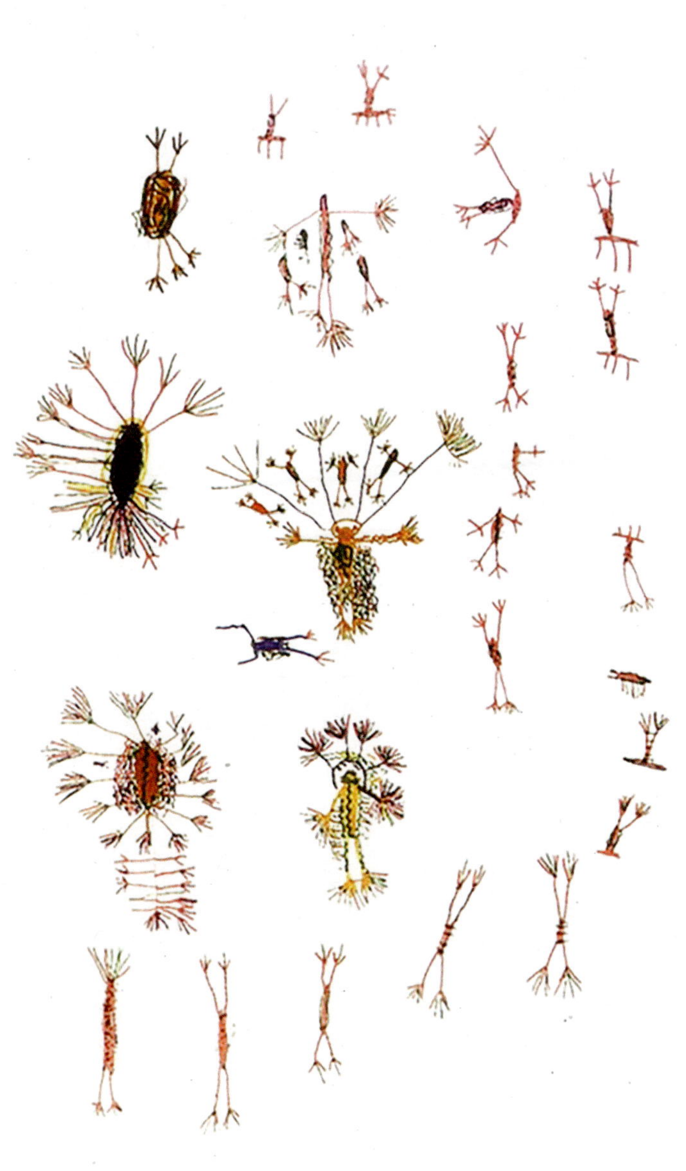

p 58 →

Laymert Garcia dos Santos

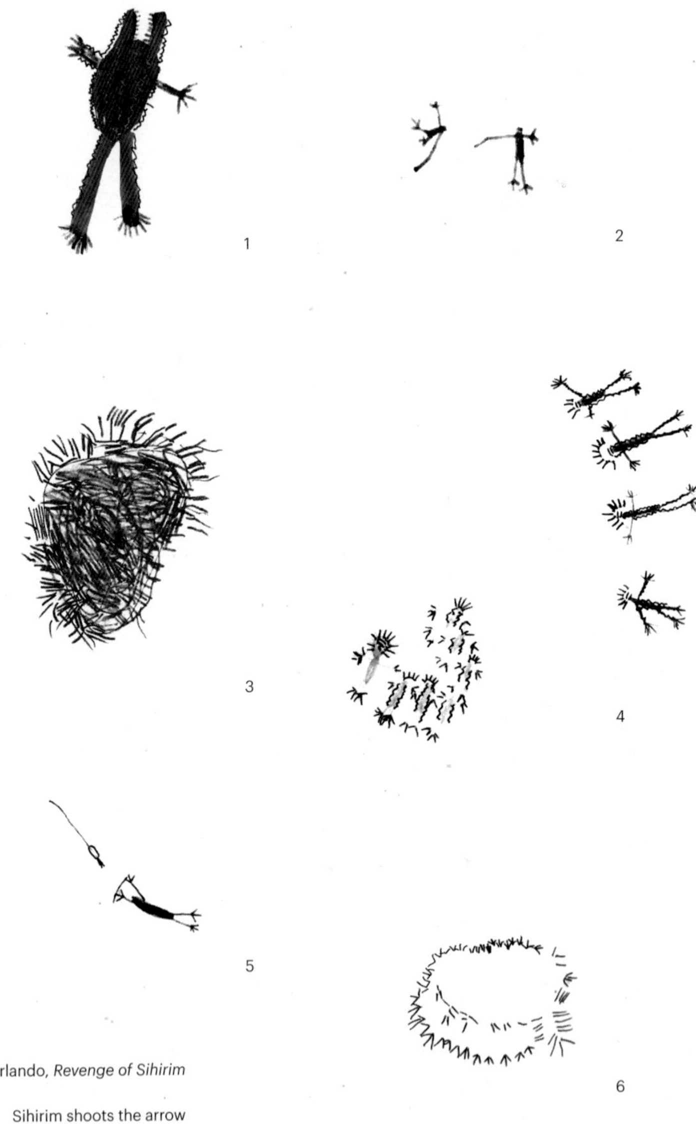

Orlando, *Revenge of Sihirim*

1 Sihirim shoots the arrow
2 Poripo is eating children
3 Children
4 A lot of blood floods generating Yanomamis
5 Yanomamis
6 Poripo sleeps in a beautiful hammock

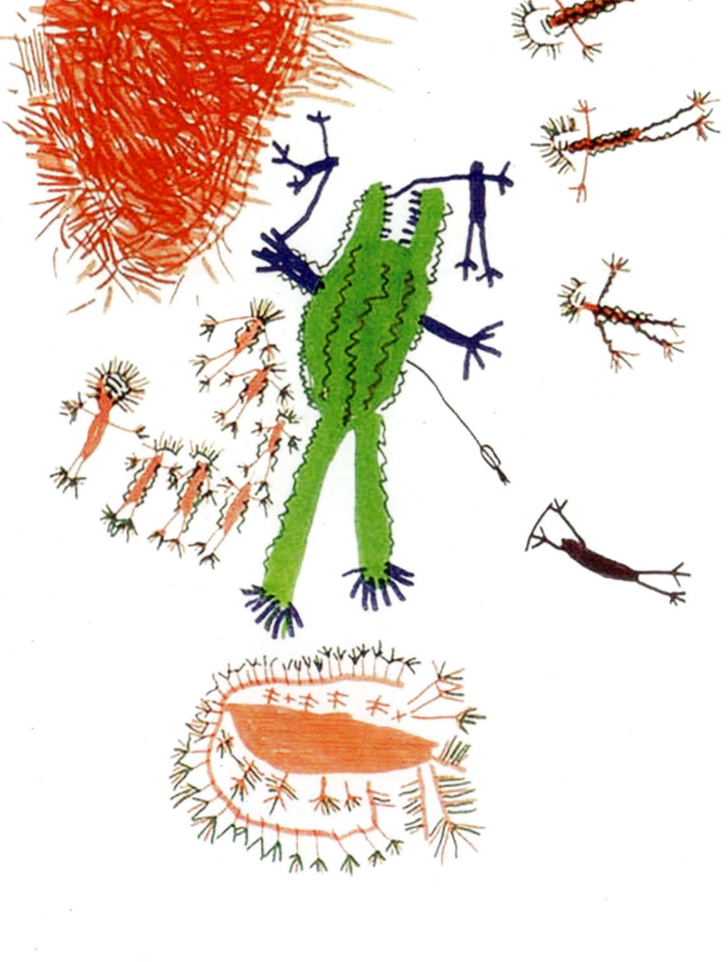

p 59 →

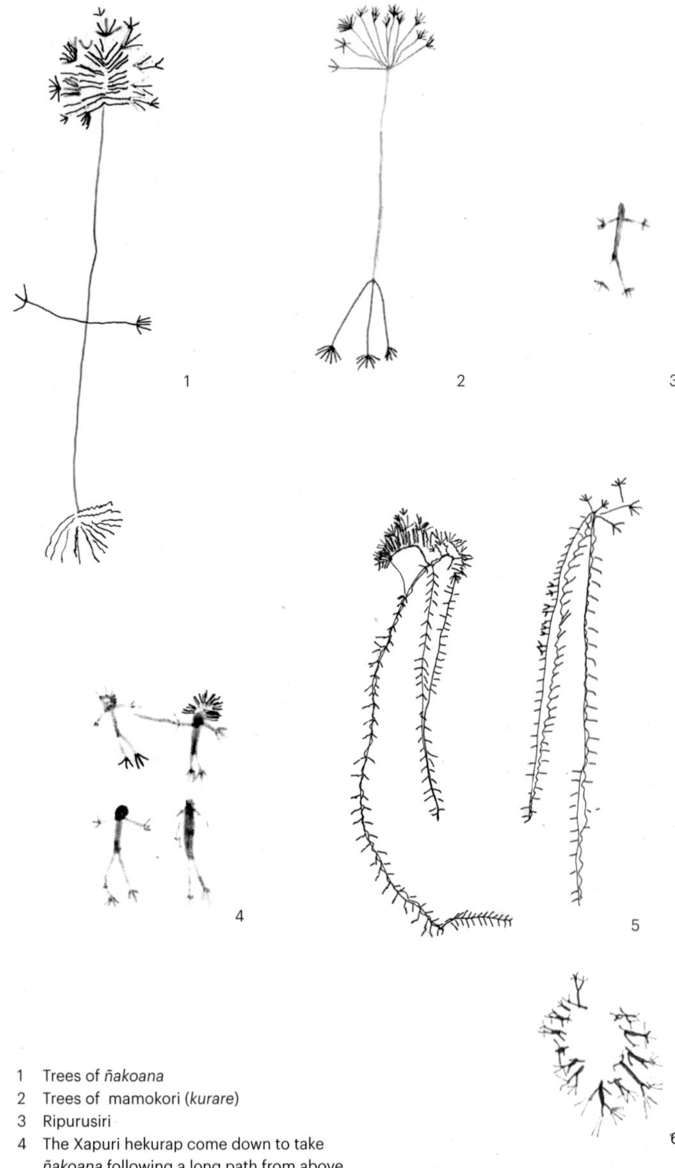

1 Trees of *ñakoana*
2 Trees of mamokori (*kurare*)
3 Ripurusiri
4 The Xapuri hekurap come down to take
 ñakoana following a long path from above
5 Paths
6 The Xapuri take the powder of the *kurare*
7 Powder of *kurare*

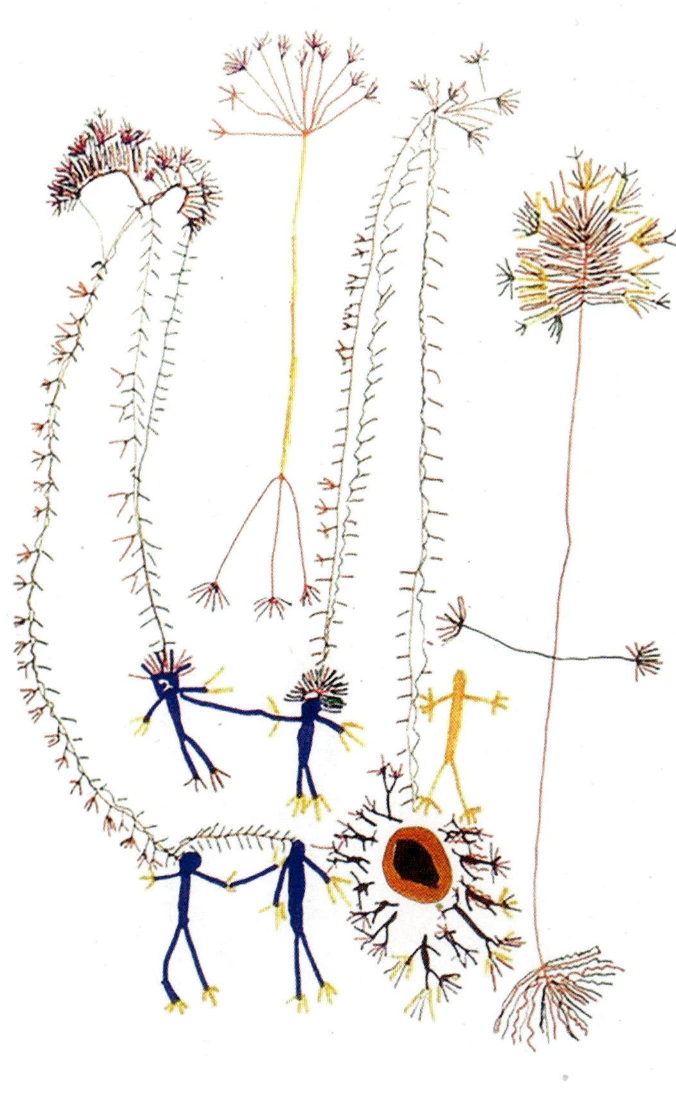

p 60 →

Laymert Garcia dos Santos

p 63 →

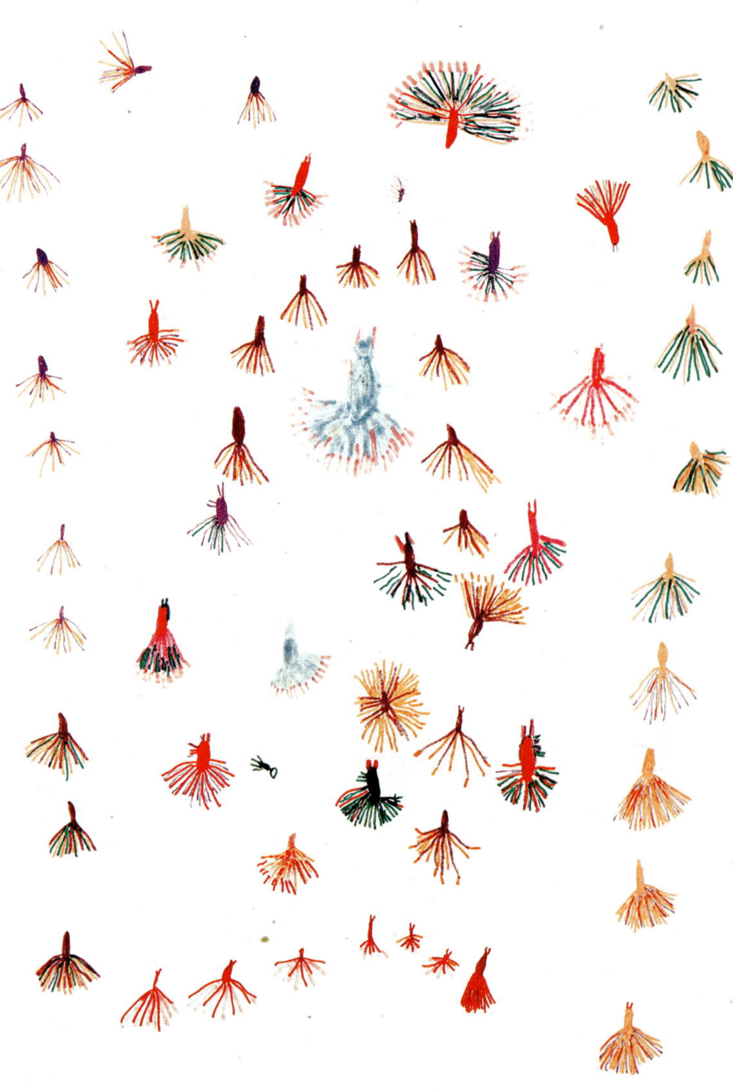

Orlando

The *mutum* (*paruri*) which symbolizes night (*titi*).
Note: This drawing was also referred to as the
descent of x*apiri pë*.

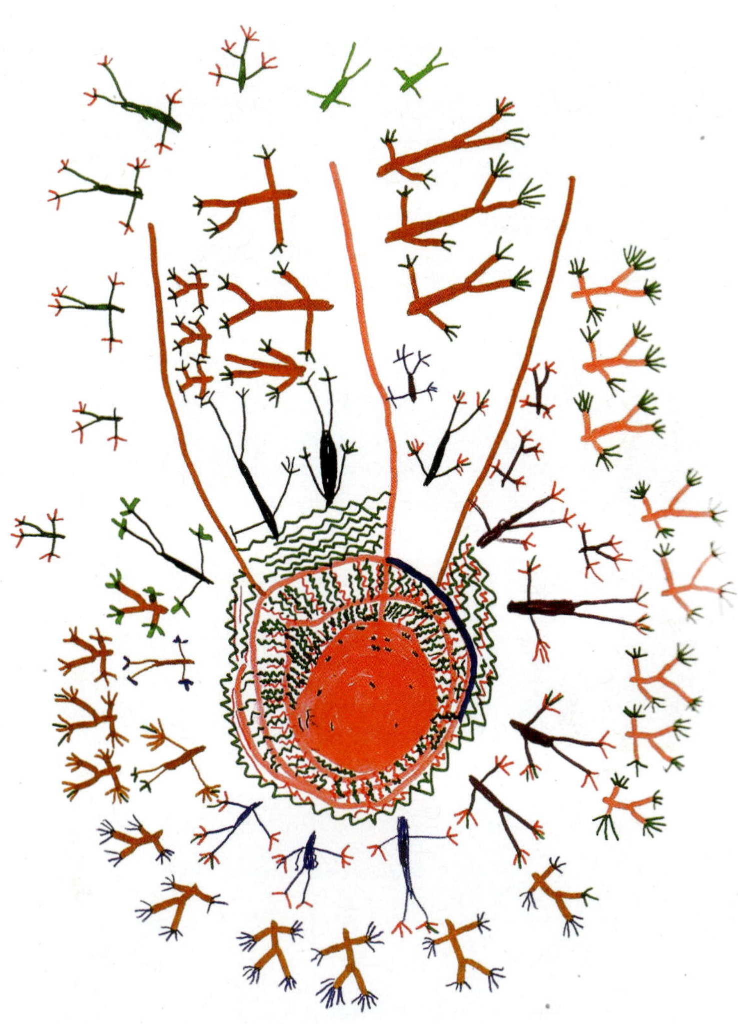

Orlando, *Motoka and sons*

p 65 →

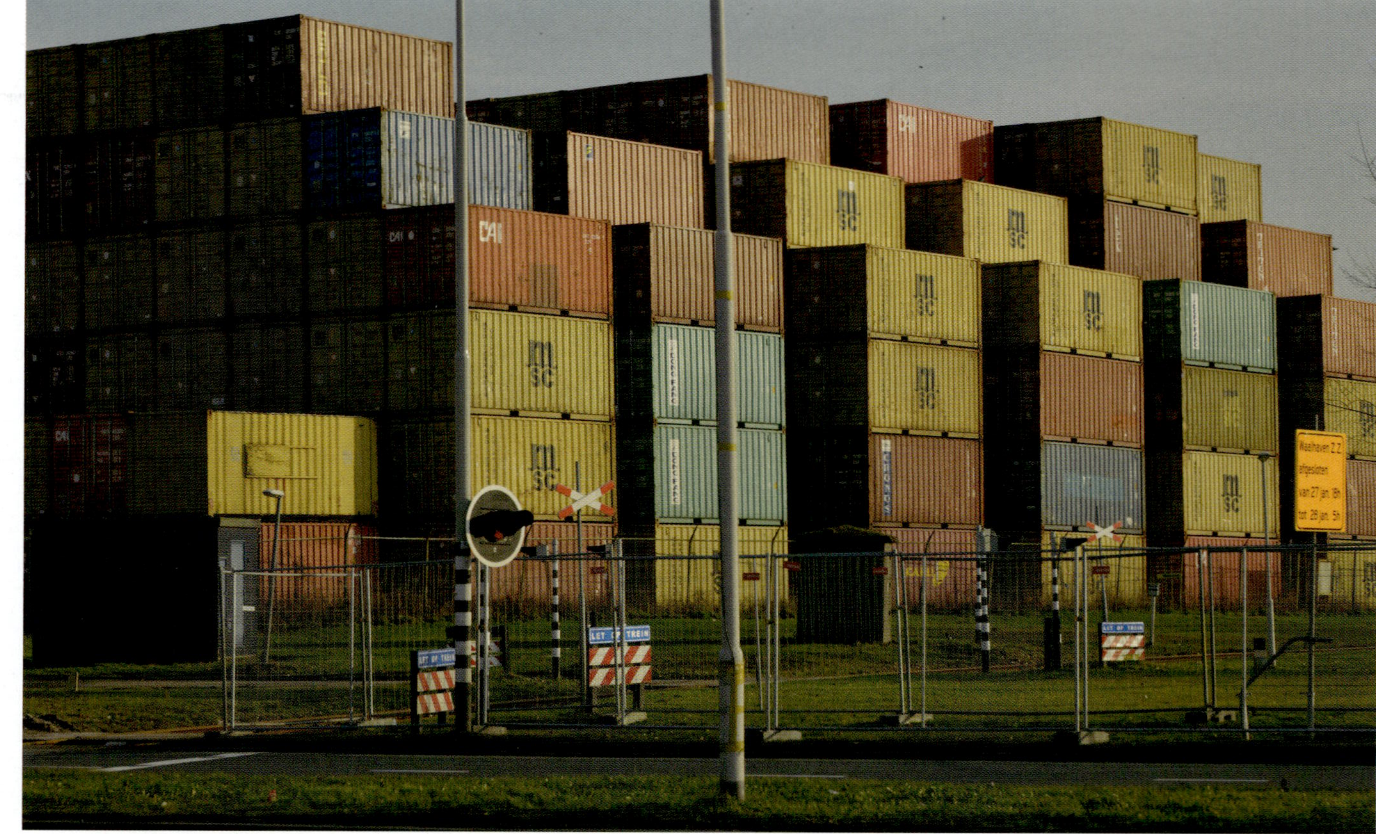

Collective Reading: Sekula, Easterling, and Harney & Moten

p 72 →

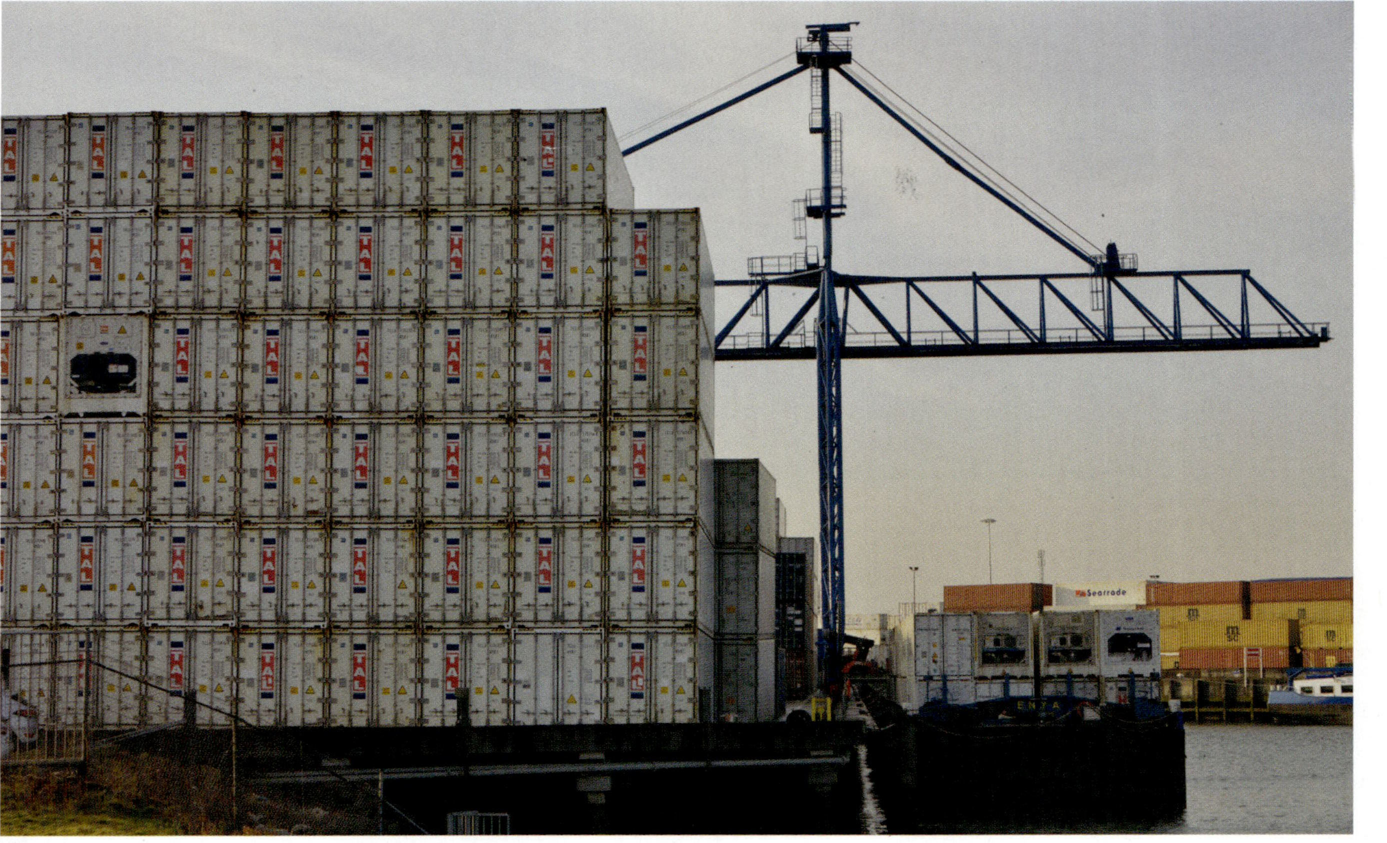

Collective Reading: Sekula, Easterling, and Harney & Moten

p 75 →

E. C. Feiss

p 77 →

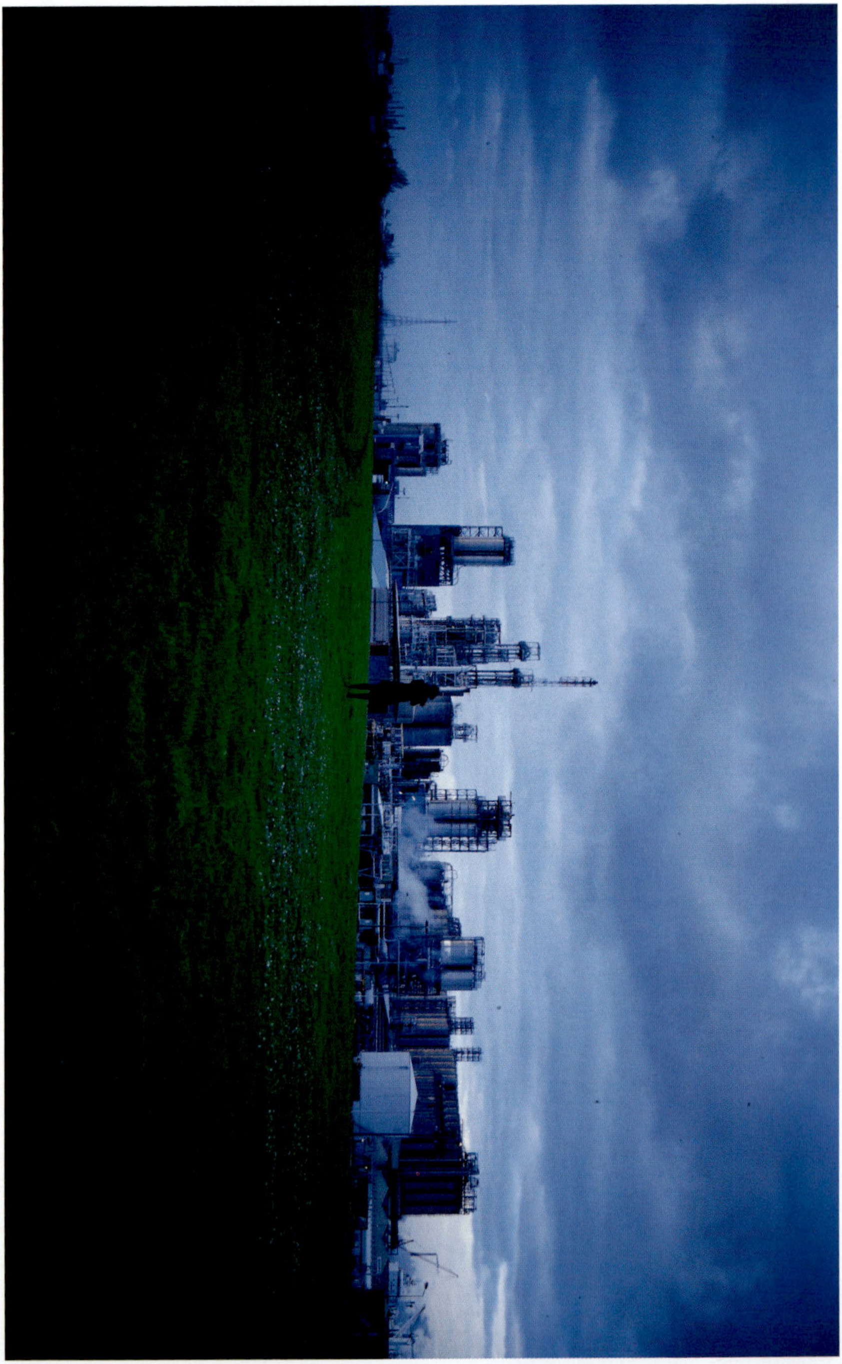

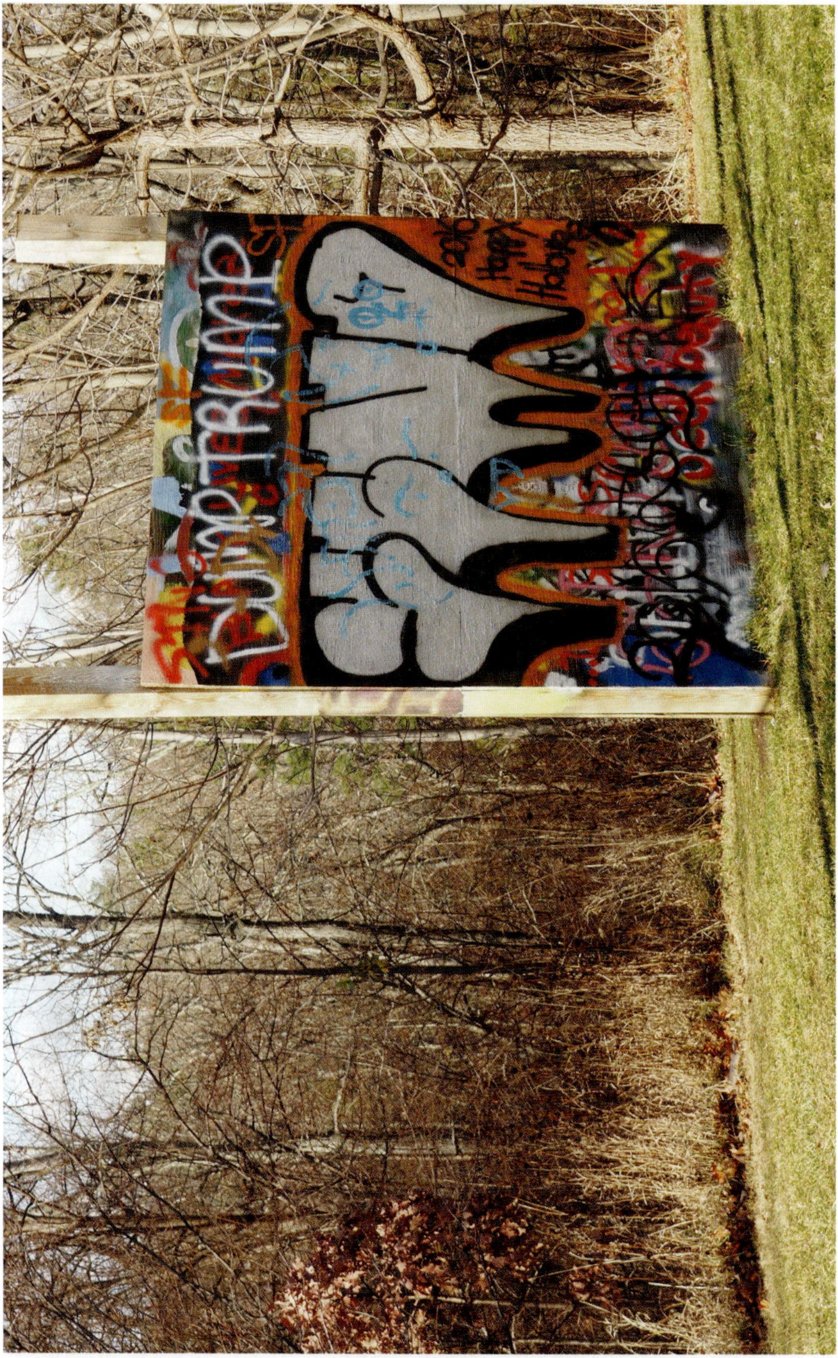

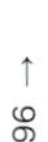

p 96 →

Sarah Pierce

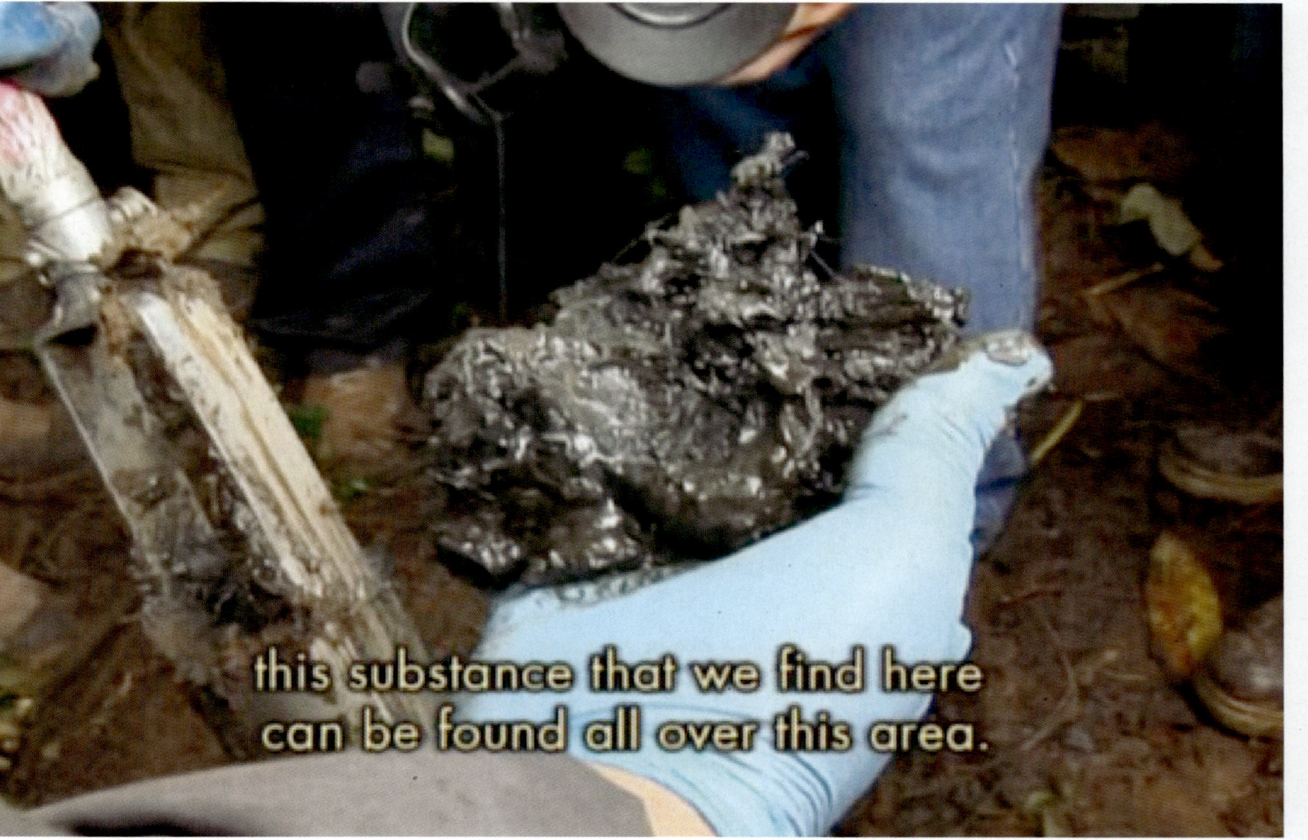
this substance that we find here
can be found all over this area.

p 102 →

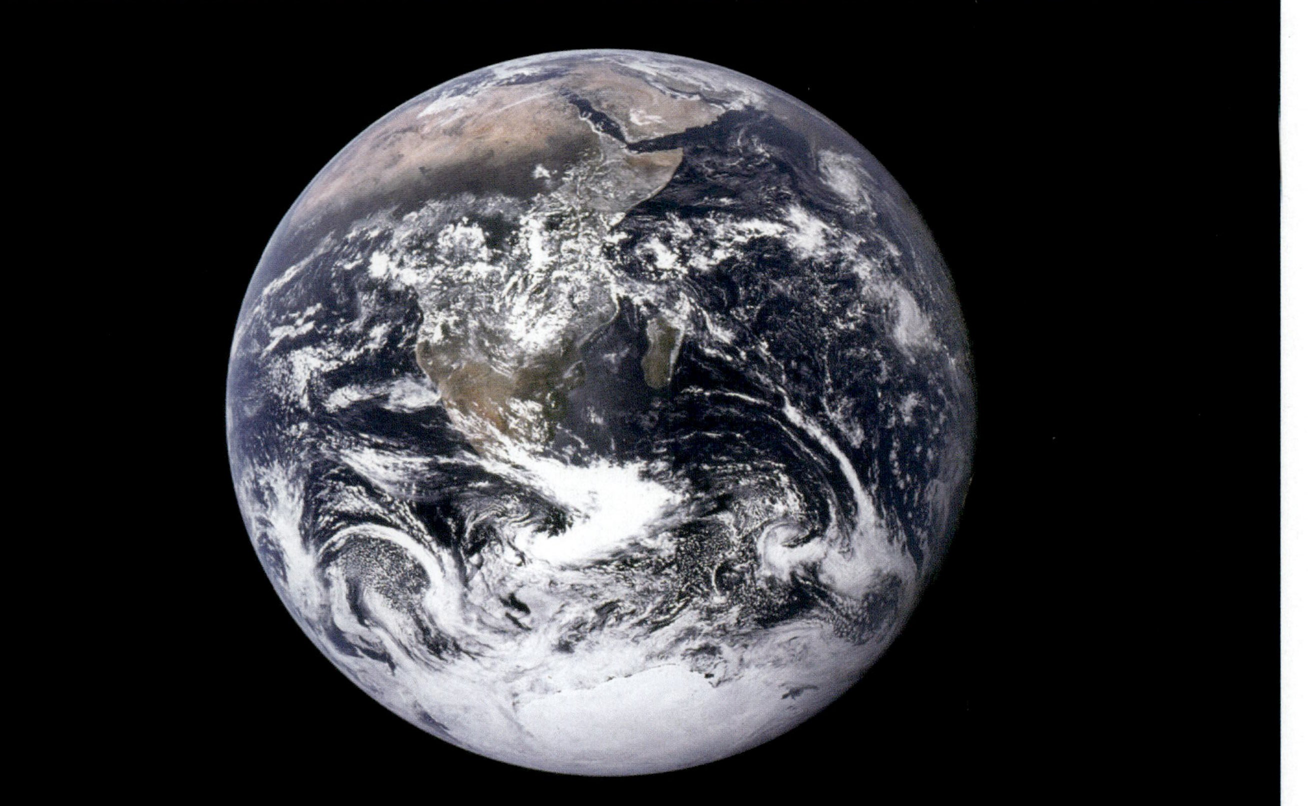

Paulo Tavares

p 103 →

Fragments in Earth Archaeology

p 104 →

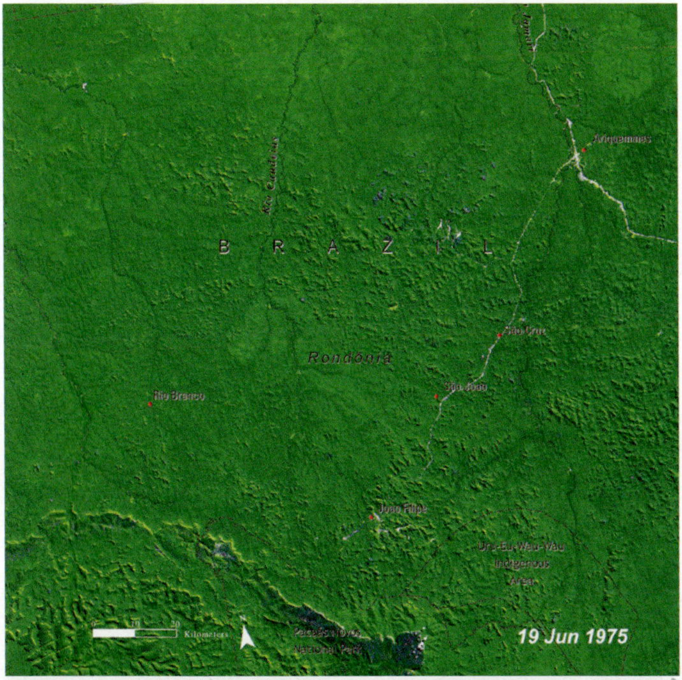

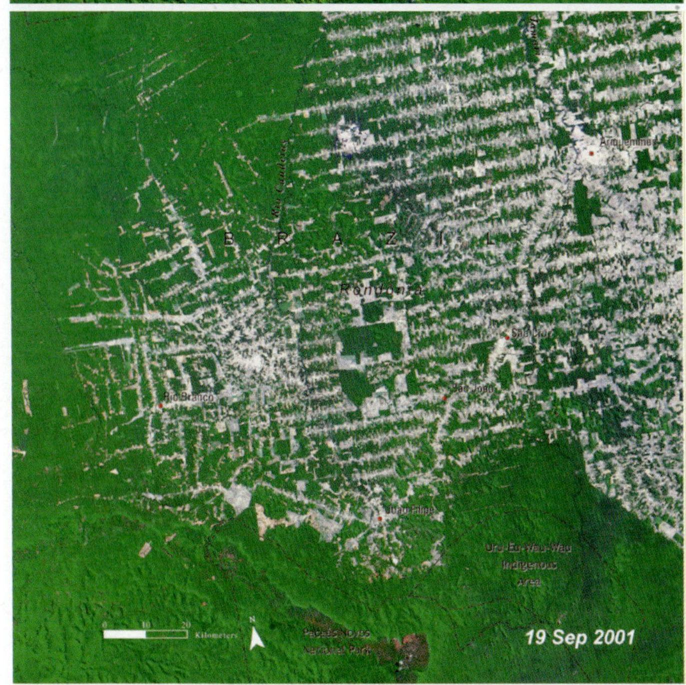

p 105 →

Paulo Tavares

p 107 →

CENTRO-ALDEIAMENTO
RIO JAUAPERY
RIO ALALAÚ
Cach. Criminosa
Acampam. A2
Caminho Y
Posto Indígena do XXI
A
B
18 S. Antônio
Acampam. A1
RIO UATUMÃ
RIO NEGRO
RIO URUBÚ
MANAUS
RIO AMAZONAS
REGIÃO RIO ALALAÚ
escala 1:2.000.000
estrada desmatada
estrada demarcada
malocas já localizadas
posto indígena
acampamentos em programa
caminho
60°
0
2°

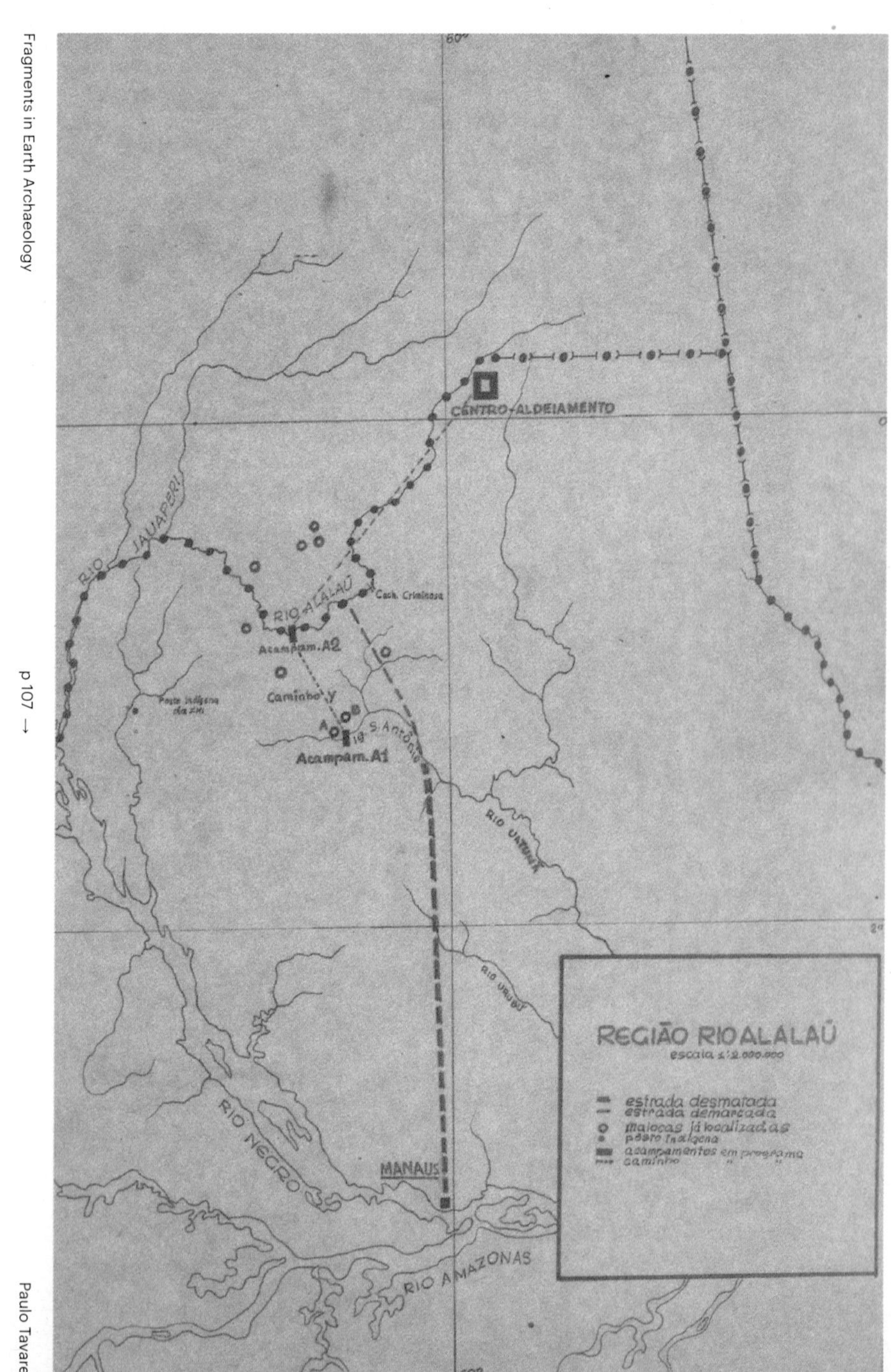

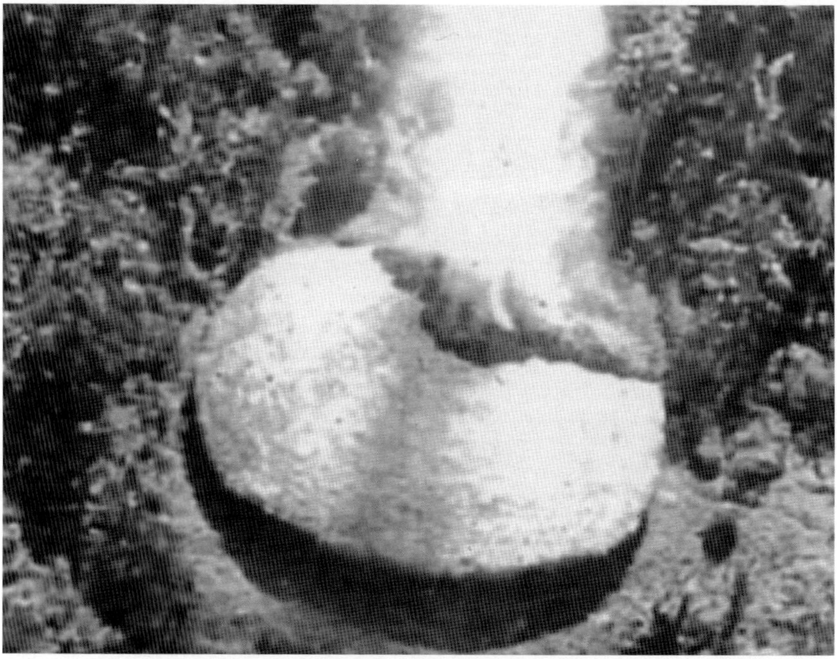

p 106, 111 →

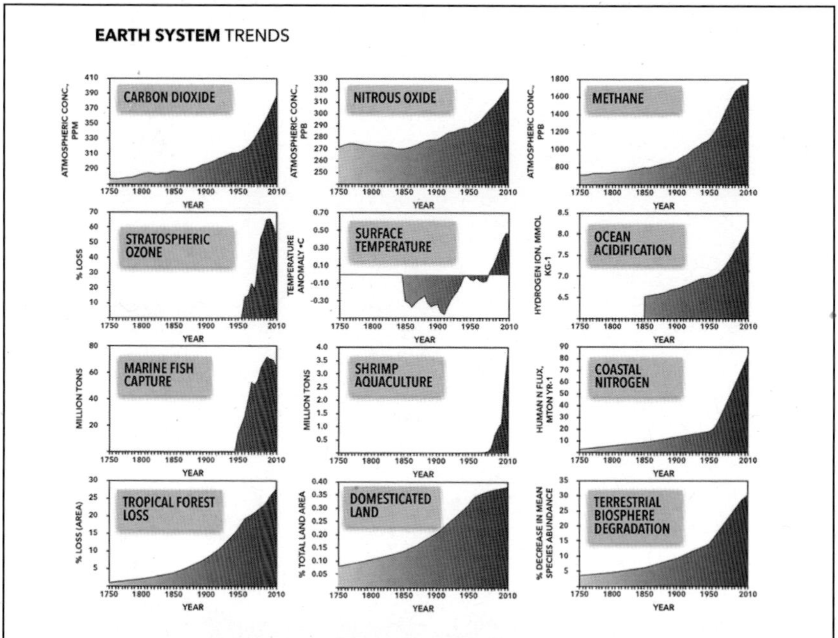

EARTH SYSTEM TRENDS

p 112 →

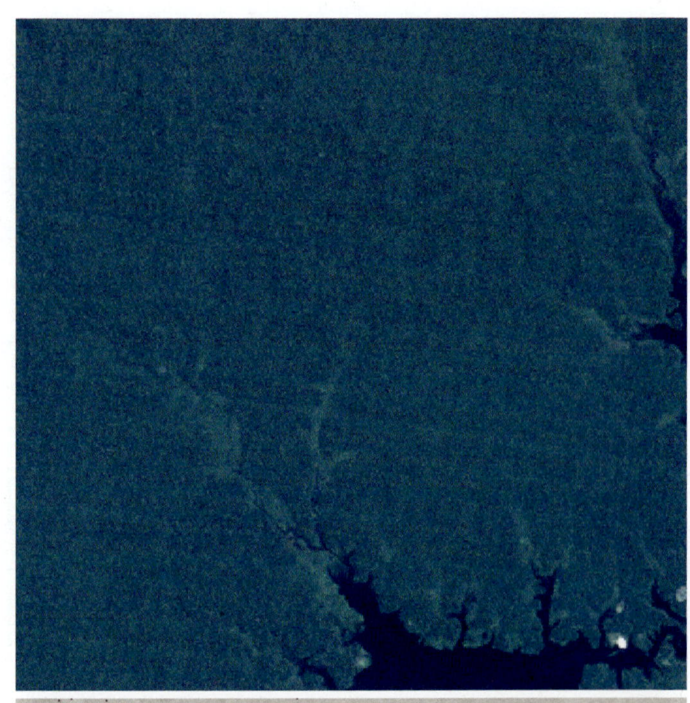

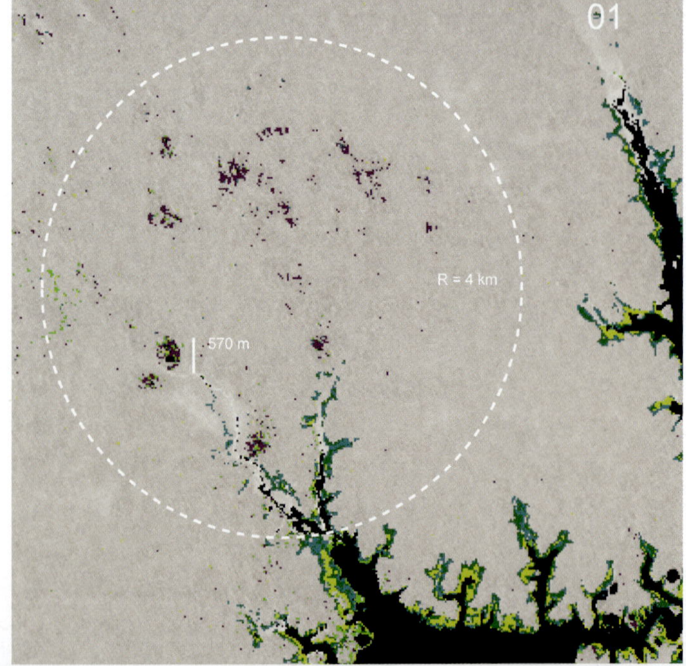

INDIGENOUS
POST DUNDAI
area under interdiction
for "pacification" · 1981
XERY
B R A Z I L
RIO ALALAÚ
area under interdiction
for "pacification" · 1974
MAIKON
POTENTIAL VILLAGE
CLUSTERS THAT EXISTED
BEFORE THE PACIFICATION
CAMPAIGN
< 6   7   10   13   14   22   23   25   > 27
           8   11   14   15   23   24   26   YEARS
                                                    OLD
OLD   NON
GROWTH   FOREST
0   2.5   5   10 km

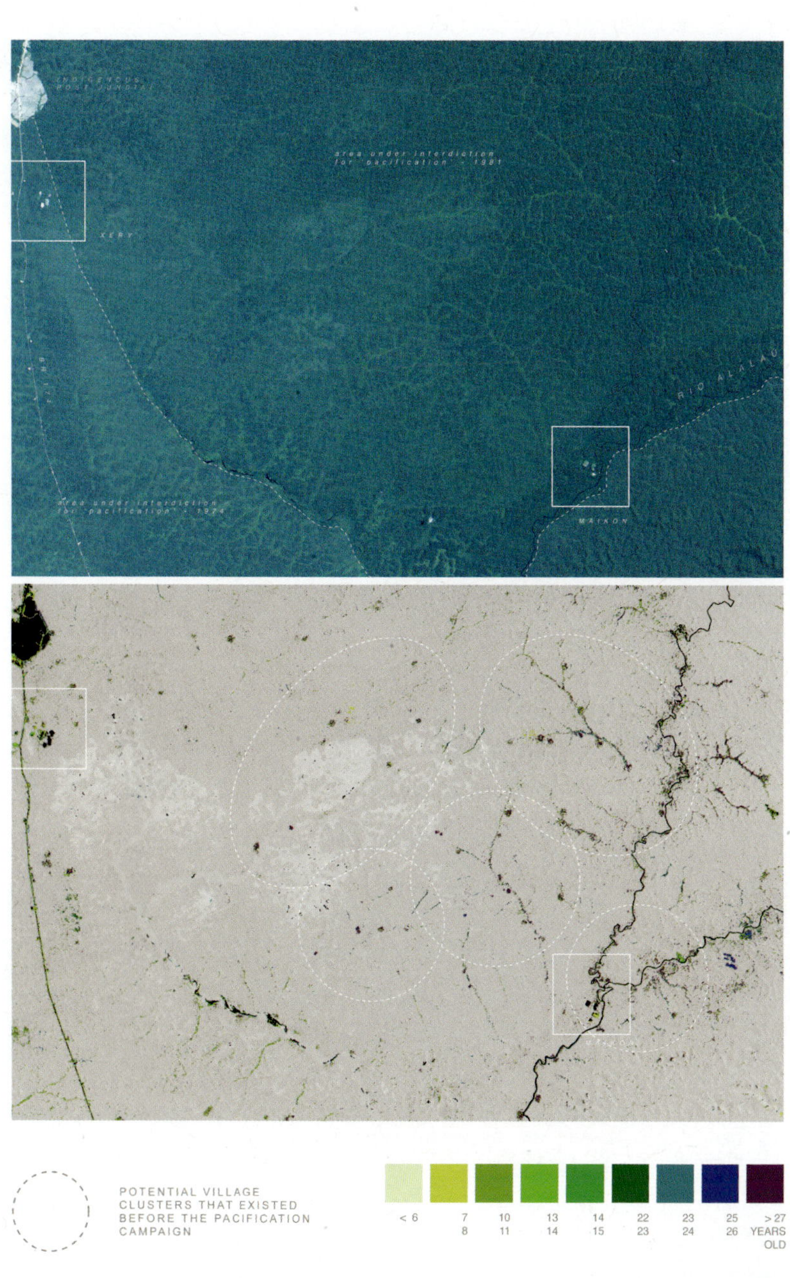

p 113 →

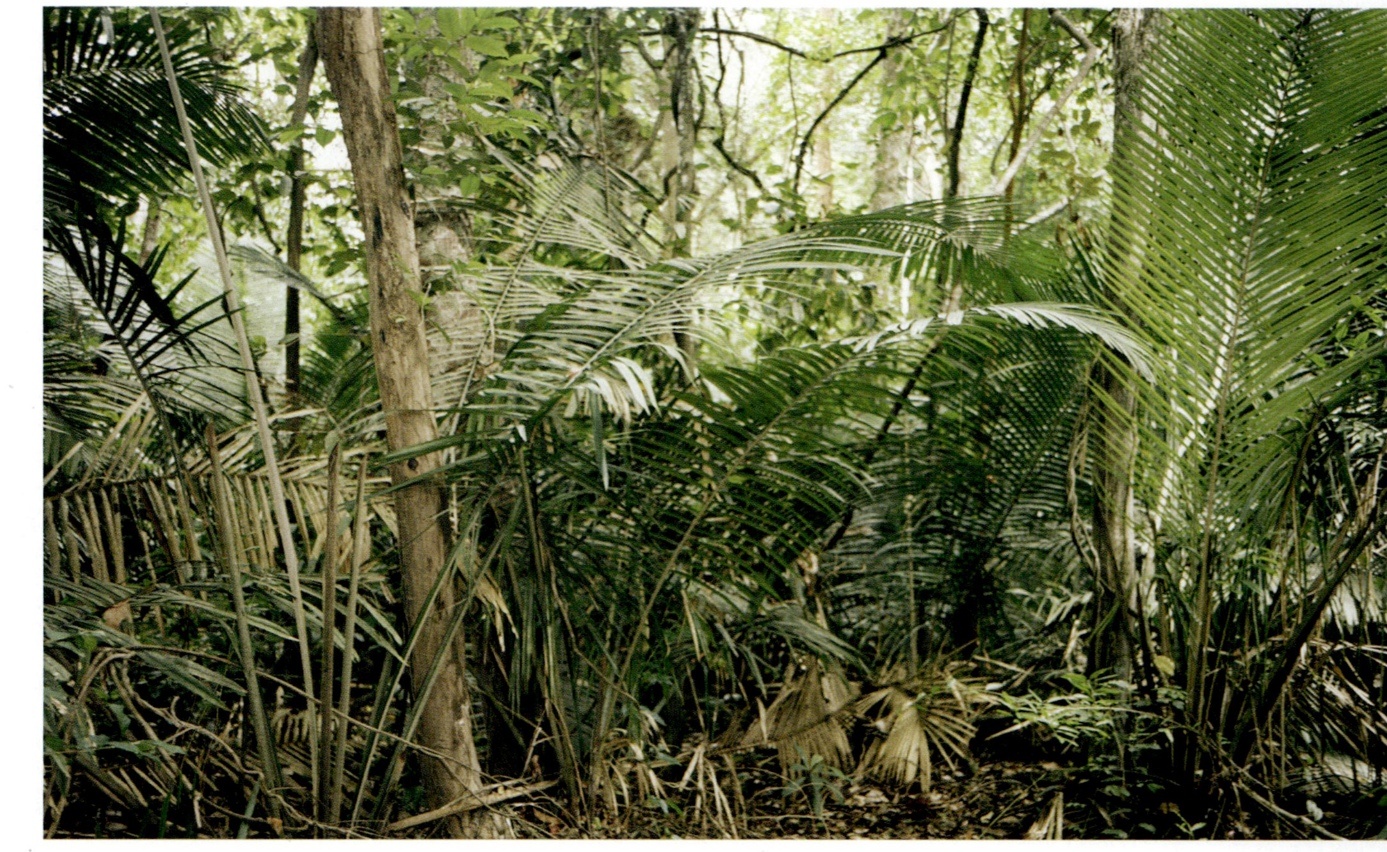

p 114 →

Paulo Tavares

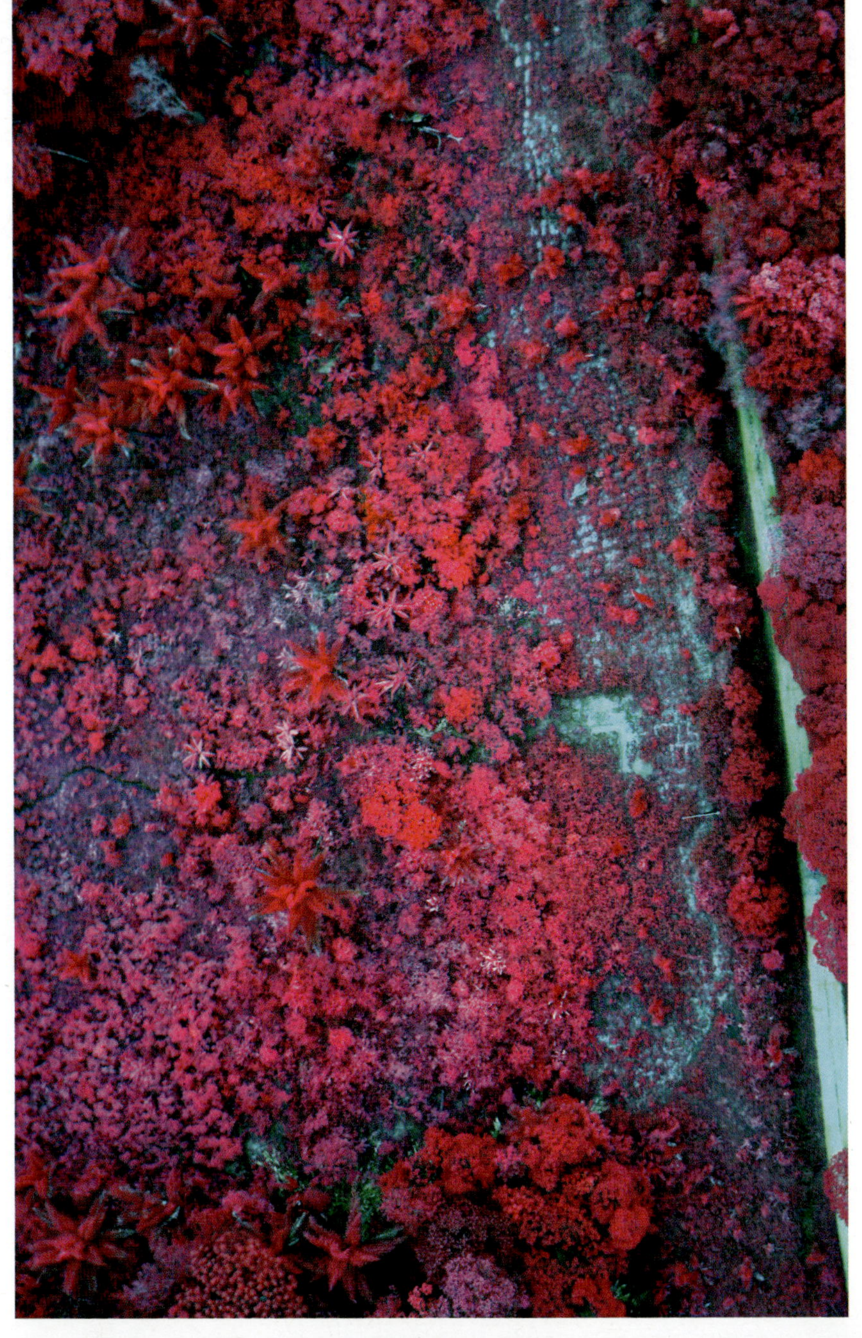

p 116 →

Paulo Tavares

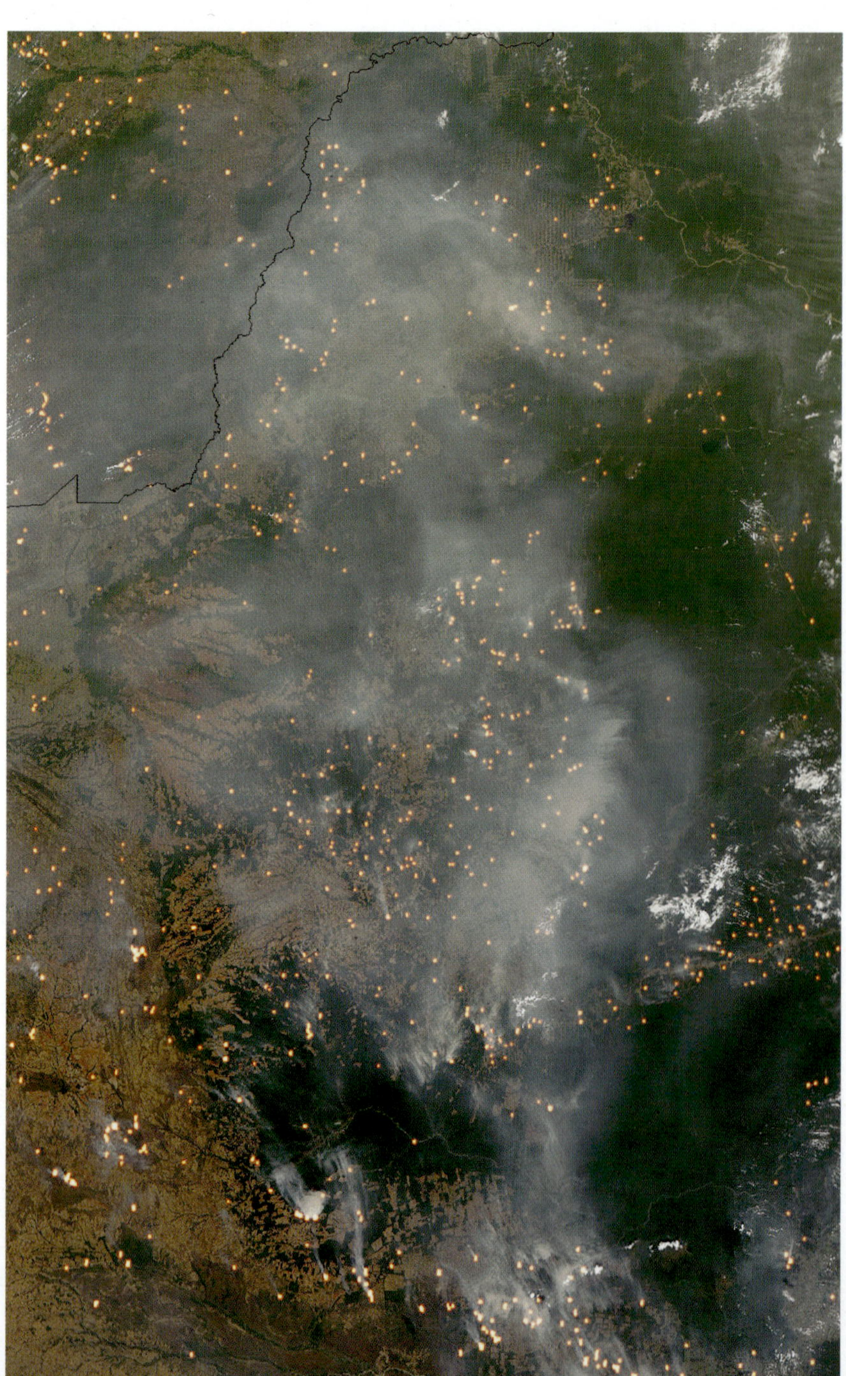

p 117 →

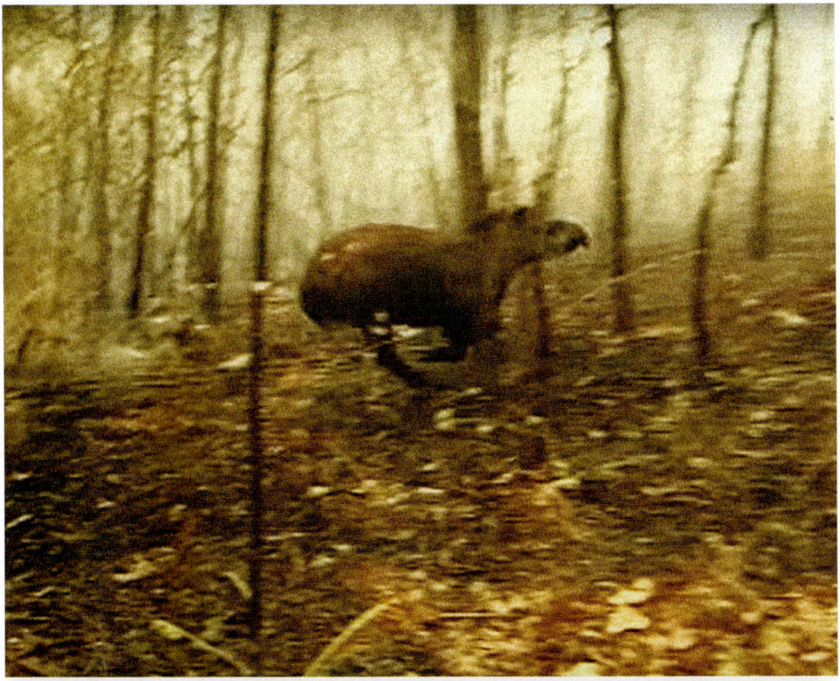

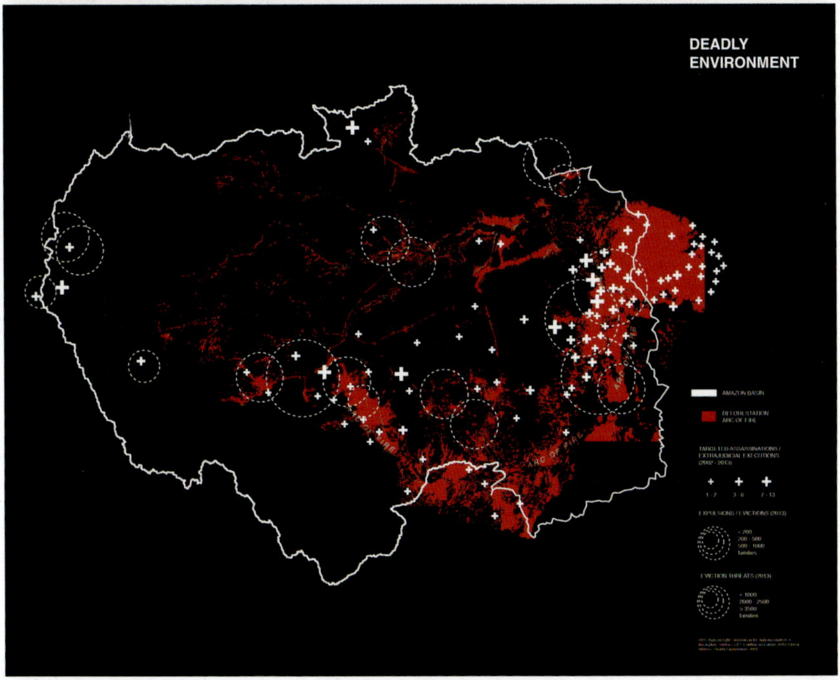

p 121, 119 →

Paulo Tavares

Glossary

193 — 201

Liz Allan is an artist and writer working with experimental video. Her palette extends to words: in print, via subtitles, and by way of voice. Her attention to authorial representation within new documentary traditions delineates a fascination with selves formed at the meeting points between subjectivities, in and out of their contexts. Born and raised in Aotearoa New Zealand, she lives and works in Rotterdam, is a member of All the Cunning Stunts, and coeditor of *A Recent Writing*.

Bik Van der Pol are Rotterdam-based artists, working collectively since 1995. They understand artistic practice as a form of learning and a process for continuous reconfiguration, using dialogue as its major mode of transfer. They co-initiated the School of Missing Studies in 2003, and were the program directors of the School of Missing Studies at the Sandberg Instituut from 2013 to 2015.

Charles Esche is a curator, writer, and director of Van Abbemuseum, Eindhoven. His work involves the theory and practice of art museums, art centers, and biennials. His writings on institutional possibility and policy are useful aids for rethinking the relation between art and social change. He was also curator of the 31st São Paulo Biennial and engaged in several dialogues with the students of the School of Missing Studies during and after the biennial.

E. C. Feiss is a writer, critic, and PhD candidate at the University of California, Berkeley, studying the history and theory of modern and contemporary art, specifically Western socially and politically engaged art practices that articulate programs for justice and social utility. She is interested in the museology of exhibiting political and protest art, and writes broadly about art after 1960. She was involved in the School of Missing Studies as a reading and writing tutor.

Laymert Garcia dos Santos is an essayist and sociologist based in São Paulo. Involved in the cultural experiment Amazonas—Music Theatre in Three Parts, this collaboration between European and Brazilian researchers, and Yanomami from Amazona presented the consequences of the destruction of the rainforest, and the relationship between the conceptual world of Indigenous magic and a Western scientific orientation. His talk during *Turning a Blind Eye* addressed the schizophrenic relationship of Brazilians toward Indigenous peoples.

Sarah Pierce is an artist based in Dublin. She holds a PhD in visual cultures from Goldsmiths College. She uses the term "The Metropolitan Complex" to describe her work. Her processes of research and presentation highlight a continual renegotiation of the terms for making art: the potential for dissent and self-determination and the proximity of past artworks. She was a core tutor at the School of Missing Studies.

Eloise Sweetman is a curator, writer, and teacher based in Rotterdam. Through her practice she investigates systems of exchange where ideas, methodologies, discussion, and materials are made active and radiate out. She works through various disciplines involving artists, philosophers, political theorists, cultural theorists, poets, architects, psychologists, and others. She graduated from the School of Missing Studies.

Paulo Tavares is a Brazilian architect, urbanist, and researcher at the project Forensic Architecture, and based in Quito. His work is concerned with the relations between conflict and space as they intersect within cities, territories, and ecologies. During the program *Turning a Blind Eye* he presented an open roundtable to discuss the relations between spatial practices, visual cultures, political ecology, and the ruins of the Anthropocene.

Nato Thompson is a writer and artistic director of Creative Time in New York, which commissions and supports socially engaged art as a way to empower communities to see power and reimagine it. He sees culture is a tool that can and does inspire innovation and dramatic transformation—perhaps as never before. In democracy, he argues, culture affects us directly and powerfully: suffusing the world we live in, influencing our emotions, actions, and very understanding of ourselves as citizens.

School of Missing Studies
Edited by Bik Van der Pol
Sandberg Series n°1
Published by Sandberg Instituut and Sternberg Press

The Sandberg Instituut is the masters program of the Gerrit Rietveld
Academie in Amsterdam (the Netherlands), and offers master's degrees
in fine arts, interior architecture, applied arts, and design. Jurgen Bey,
director since 2010, has sought to align the institute with the dynamics
of contemporary society. He introduced one-off, two-year programs
developed in relationship to urgent global issues. These temporary
programs form an intense "insertion" in the Sandberg Instituut,
challenging and influencing the regular programs in different ways, with
the ultimate aim to develop education and learning further from within
the institution. To create a record of the temporary programs and as a
platform for critical reflection on what temporality could potentially bring
to an institute of continuous education, as well as to society at large,
the Sandberg Instituut initiated the Sandberg Series, which focuses on
changes in art education and in which the issues and urgencies of each
of the programs are put forward and reflected upon.

The School of Missing Studies, led by artists Bik Van der Pol, is the
second temporary master program at the Sandberg Instituut. The School
of Missing Studies is also an ongoing project in collaboration with artists,
thinkers, and architects, initiated by Bik Van der Pol, Srdjan Janović
Weiss, and Sabine von Fischer in 2003. Since its initiation, the School of
Missing Studies has functioned as a nomadic, collaborative platform for
experimental study and research on the public environment, which is
currently undergoing abrupt transitions. Under the roof of the Sandberg
Instituut the project operated from 2013 to 2015, as a one-off masters
program.

Students: Abla elBahrawy, Clare Butcher, Sofia Caesar, Sanne Cobussen,
Katinka de Jonge, Nikola Knežević, Grace Kyne-Lilley, Mariana Lanari,
Geert van Mil, Dina Rončević, Eloise Sweetman, Meir Tati, Luisa Ungar

Tutors and guests: Lawrence Abu Hamdan, Nick Aikens, Ayreen Anastas
and Rene Gabri, Samira Ben Laloua, Bik Van der Pol, Maria Boletsi,
Jeremiah Day, Charles Esche, E. C. Feiss, Louis van Gasteren,
Moosje Goosen, Ernst van den Hemel, Pamela M. Lee, Maria Lind,
Sven Lütticken, Sarah Pierce, Tina Sherwell, Matthew Stadler,
Nomeda & Gediminas Urbonas, Alexander Premala Vollebregt,
Jeroen Zuidgeest

Program coordinator: Martine Zoeteman

School of Missing Studies
Edited by Bik Van der Pol
Sandberg Series n°1
Published by Sandberg Instituut and Sternberg Press

Authors: Liz Allan, Bik Van der Pol, Charles Esche, E. C. Feiss,
Laymert Garcia dos Santos, Sarah Pierce, Eloise Sweetman,
Paulo Tavares, Nato Thompson
Associate editor and copy editor: Liz Allan
Proofreader: Marnie Slater
Designer: Anja Groten
Printing: BUD Potsdam
Coordination Sandberg Series: Sjoerd ter Borg

Acknowledgements: Marjo van Baar, Oliver Barstow, Jurgen Bey,
Femke Dekker, Tatjana Günthner, Antje Klaster, Jaap Vinken,
Nancy van Vooren, Caroline Schneider, Anke Zedelius
First edition, 2017
ISBN 978-3-95679-331-8
Published by Sandberg Instituut and Sternberg Press

Sandberg Instituut
Masters of Art and Design
Fred. Roeskestraat 98
NL-1076 ED Amsterdam
www.sandberg.nl

Sternberg Press
Caroline Schneider
Karl-Marx-Allee 78
D-10243 Berlin
www.sternberg-press.com

Sandberg Instituut

Sternberg Press

Sandberg Series

School of Missing Studies
Sandberg Series n°1
Edited by Bik Van der Pol
Sandberg Instituut (Amsterdam)
Sternberg Press (Berlin), 2017
ISBN 978-3-95679-331-8

Eternal Erasure—On Fashion Matters
Sandberg Series n°2
Edited by Pieter Van Bogaert, Martine Zoeteman,
& Christophe Coppens
Sandberg Instituut (Amsterdam)
Sternberg Press (Berlin), 2017
ISBN 978-3-95679-342-4

Material Utopias
Sandberg Series n°3
Edited by Louise Schouwenberg
Sandberg Instituut (Amsterdam)
Sternberg Press (Berlin), 2017
ISBN 978-3-95679-343-1